THE SNARE IS BROKEN

A JOURNEY TO FREEDOM

FROM THE GRIP OF

SEXUAL ABUSE AND PORNOGRAPHY

Bruce D. Hughes
God is doing a new thing!
Isa. 43:18-19

BRUCE D. HUGHES, Ph.D.

The Snare is Broken
A Journey From the Grip of Sexual Abuse and Pornography
by Bruce D. Hughes Ph.D.

Printed in the United States of America

ISBN 9781612154749

Unless otherwise indicated, Bible quotations are taken from The King James Version.

www.xulonpress.com

Table of Contents

Part Two: Consequences and Victory

Acknowledgement

It is my privilege to acknowledge and give praise to Dr. Timothy Bryant of Cornerstone Family Health in Williamsport, Pennsylvania. His counsel, guidance and teaching during the first six years of my ordeal have left a lasting impact. Peggy and I will always be indebted to him for being available for God's service and for his compassionate spirit.

He was willing to step outside the normal short-term intensive care he usually provides to his clients. His support helped me to move beyond the victim that I had become over the years and into a place of victory. His wise counsel led me from a place of devastation to one where I found peace and joy. I will be eternally grateful to him.

Dedication

This book is dedicated to my beloved wife, Peggy, our two sons, Patrick and Michael, and their wives, Debbie and Sue. Except for the Lord Himself, these five people are largely responsible for lifting me up and giving me strength through the life-changing experience described in the pages that follow.

Peggy, you are one of a kind for sure. So many other wives would have sent their husbands packing, but you always encouraged and defended me and stood beside me, even when I wasn't very lovable. I know there were many times when you were hurt by my depressed moods and angry tones, but you never gave up on me. I'll always love you for it.

Patrick and Debbie, Michael and Sue, your love and support meant more to me than you will ever know. I was so fearful that you would pull away from me because of my legal and moral mistakes. Instead, you each drew close to me and gave me courage to carry on each day. Thank you, too, for pressing me to write this book so that others may benefit from the lessons I have learned.

INTRODUCTION

There are numerous references in the Bible to snares, traps or nets. These are references to Satan's methods of trapping people so that they become his captives and slaves, rather than being devoted to their creator God. He baits his snares with whatever he knows will entrap each individual person. "*But every man is tempted, when he is drawn away of his own lust, and enticed.*" *James 1:14*

Life is fraught with pain and heartache for nearly everyone. Few are exempt from some form of hurt, suffering, or regret during their lifetime. Broken relationships, physical and emotional pain, career losses, financial woes, and a host of other struggles bring people to their knees. Sometimes these burdens are endured for years, never allowing a person to become what God intended them to be.

Like many people in today's world, I experienced sexual abuse as a child. Unlike many, I have found peace. However, before I found that peace I endured years of torment that led to ending a successful career in humiliating public disgrace. This book reveals both my struggles and the path I traveled to break free from the snare that had entrapped me.

At age fifty-five, the story of my abuse and its impact on me became known to the public. I had engaged in behavior on the Internet that led to having my story in the headlines of the local newspapers. At first I was devastated, but once my secret was out, I received encouraging words from people who had also been abused. Some people informed me that I was the first person to whom they had ever told their story. Others remarked that my willingness to talk about my childhood abuse and to seek help had given them the strength and courage to move out of their own comfort zones and begin to deal with their past and all the deeply buried emotions that went along with it.

As I talked to a Christian counselor about my abuse and its impact, I found a release from my struggles that I never thought possible. He helped me see myself as Christ sees me. He led me through a process that focused on my view of my abusers, beliefs about myself, and most importantly, my relationship with Christ. I reached a point where all I wanted to do was talk about the new freedom I felt in Christ.

My wife cautioned me that I should consider the possibility that people might not want to hear my story as much as I wanted to tell it. But I couldn't help talking about what had been bottled up inside me for so many years. What had been painful, bitter memories became living proof of God's grace toward me.

Satan is intent on snaring as many people in his traps as he can, Christians and non-Christians alike. I was not a Christian when my abuse occurred, but, after I became a Christian, Satan ensnared me in his net of guilt and bitterness that continuously interfered with my relationship with Christ. It is my hope that through learning about my life struggles and the method God used to answer my pleas to be rescued from Satan's snare, others might be convinced that they do not have to live in bondage to their past or present sins, whatever they may be.

You don't have to be trapped in your personal world of hurt. God has promised that "*...the snare is broken, and we are escaped.*" *Psalm 124:7*

This book is divided into two parts with an interlude between them. Part One is about my life from the time of my sexual abuse and its impact on me until I was about fifty-four years of age. The Interlude describes the period of eighteen to twenty-four months when I became overwhelmed with depression leading to very bad choices. Finally, Part Two describes the events after my sinful habit with Internet pornography was discovered and I was prosecuted for possession of child pornography. Most importantly, it describes God's amazing rescue plan and His path to set me free from Satan's snare.

PART ONE

SEXUAL ABUSE AND THE IMPACT

Chapter 1

COURT APPEARANCE FOR SENTENCING

On August 29, 2005, I sat at the defendant's table in the federal courtroom in Williamsport, Pennsylvania. The silence that enveloped the wood-paneled room, with its indirect lighting and high-tech electronic equipment, was bone-chilling. The distinguished, white-haired judge in his black robe leaned back in his elevated throne-like position.

The court staff sat at a lower level in front of him. A representative from the Federal Probation Department sat across the room, leafing through the pages of a folder. Two news reporters waited off to one side with pens poised. Ten members of my family and one close friend sat behind me, giving me reassuring smiles and facial expressions that seemed to say, "I'm so sorry."

My attorney sat beside me in silence. His stern look concerned me and made me think that perhaps he was expecting bad news from the judge. Over the three and a half years that I had worked with him I had come to realize that he was often the bearer of bad news for me.

I thought back over the years and all the events that had brought me to this point in my life. I was about to be sentenced for one count of possession of child pornography, a charge that neither I, nor anyone who knew me, would have ever expected. I had confessed to visiting a website that contained that material, but while I knew it was morally wrong when I did it, I had no idea it was illegal. The images in question were on my computer screen, but I had never attempted to keep them or to "possess" them in the manner in which I understood that term.

It was ten minutes past the hour and the federal prosecutor had not yet arrived. The judge scowled as he glanced at the clock and then at the papers in front of him. He asked one of his staff to come closer to him, and he whispered something while shaking his head in a disapproving way. The staff member left the room.

My heart beat faster as it occurred to me that perhaps the prosecutor's absence was going to be God's way of rescuing me from the sentence that was about to be pronounced. If the prosecutor failed to show up, the judge might dismiss the charge. That was what my wife and I had prayed for more than three years.

The court staff member returned to the courtroom and whispered something to the judge. Again, the judge looked frustrated. He then announced that there had been a mix-up in scheduling in the prosecutor's office and that he would be arriving shortly.

As I sat in the cold silence, I continued to reflect on the events that had led me to that courtroom. I thought about the sexual abuse I had endured as a child and how, as a result of those experiences, Satan had kept me ensnared in his web of deception. I had spent years in misery and loneliness, feeling dirty and worthless.

The words of two of my abusers echoed through my mind. Though forty-seven years had elapsed, I could still hear them clearly saying, "You're nothing but a dirty, worthless loser." I thought this court action was about to prove that they were right.

Chapter 2

SEXUAL ABUSE EXPERIENCES

Preschool Age Abuse

Until I was six years old, my family lived on a dairy farm. My father employed farm hands who lived in a tenant house across the dirt road from our house. One time, there was a large family living there who had small children and teenage sons. One of the teenage sons had an old car which he drove around on the back roads and on our large farm. He used to coax me into his car by promising me gum and candy. However, there was more to it. Before I could get the treats, he asked me to touch him in a sexual way and he in turn touched me. At first, it was just on the outside of our clothing, but eventually led to removal of clothing. He would drive out in the fields and encourage me to engage in this behavior with him and then give me the promised gum or candy. He called me his "buddy" or "little buddy." He told me that this was what buddies did.

The innocence of childhood is a precious gift from God. Our minds are like blank slates waiting to be written on or dry sponges ready to absorb the slightest drop of moisture. In those early years we are naïve and easily influenced by adults or older children. We can be convinced that actions most adults would consider wrong are actually alright, even desirable. Professionals in the field of child development have shown that preschool children are preoccupied with seeking whatever makes them happy. They are the center of their own universe.

Today, I know that what I experienced was sexual abuse, but at that point in my young life I was convinced by the perpetrator that what he did, and what he enticed me to do to him, were perfectly normal. He told me I was his "little buddy" and that buddies kept secrets from everyone else. I don't think anyone suspected that anything wrong was happening. He never caused me any physical pain that would make me run and tell my parents. In fact, the reward of the candy and the physical pleasure I received from his touch made me want to keep the secret.

I saw him interact with his younger brothers and sisters in the same manner that he did with me, which confirmed his assurances that his behavior toward me was normal. They all seemed perfectly comfortable with it. It never occurred to me that even though I had two older brothers at home, none of that type of behavior happened there.

After about a year, the perpetrator moved away. I did not see him again until I was an adolescent. During my years in elementary school, I had no more experiences such as I had with that person. I believe that, if nothing else had happened to me, my life would have progressed normally.

Preadolescent Abuse

During the summer between sixth and seventh grade, I went on my first Boy Scout campout. Two boys were assigned to each tent. My tent partner was supposed to be a longtime friend who was the same age as me. Unfortunately, he became ill and was unable to go on the camping trip.

After we had pitched all the tents, one of the scout leaders told me I was going to have to sleep in a tent with two older boys. He escorted me to their tent, pulled back the tent flap, and yelled, "Move over, boys, you're getting an extra bunkmate tonight."

Both boys protested strongly, trying to convince the scout leader that there wasn't enough room for one more person. The leader said sarcastically, "Would you rather have me in there with you?" With that, he threw my sleeping bag and pillow into the tent and walked away.

I didn't know either of the boys very well. One of them was fifteen and the other was thirteen. Since I was twelve, their ages weren't that different from mine. However, both of them were past puberty and I hadn't even started the physiological changes that come with that phenomenon. They were taller and heavier than I and much more knowledgeable about life.

They already had their sleeping bags zipped together to function like a double bed. Their duffle bags sat on each side of the opening of the tent.

"You'll have to put your sleeping bag at our feet," one boy said.

"And you better get right to sleep if you know what's good for ya," snarled the other.

I had heard the older scouts talking at our meetings about how they played cards by flashlight, told jokes, and laughed half the night until the scout leaders threatened them if they didn't quiet down and get to sleep. My two tent mates acted as though none of that was true.

I crawled into my sleeping bag at their feet, my face next to the tent flap. As I lay there, my body trembled and I fought back tears. I wanted to go home.

I tried to not make a sound, but apparently the other two heard my sighs. They whispered and laughed. Then one of them said, "What's the matter, little boy, do you want your mommy?"

My mind raced for an answer. "I'm freezing," I said.

Again they whispered and laughed, but this time they moved some of their gear. "If you're real good," the older one said, "you can sleep with us. We'll keep you warm," he said laughing.

"Really?" I said sitting up. "Where should I put my sleeping bag?"

"You won't need it," the younger boy replied. "The way we sleep, there's room enough for all three of us."

As I started toward them, they pulled back the top cover of their bag and slid apart, opening a space between them. "Get right down in here," the older boy said. "We'll get you warmed up."

I felt a certain degree of fear, but also joy. Perhaps this was going to be a good campout after all.

Once I was under the top cover, the older boy reminded me that he had said I could sleep with them if I was good. "It's time to see how good you are."

I had no idea what he meant.

The boys touched me and told me where they wanted me to touch them. I thought back to my preschool days and the person who'd called me his "little buddy." Apparently, this really is what buddies do, I thought. I was too afraid and intimidated to even think of resisting.

What followed was severe abuse. By the time they were finished with me, I lay sobbing and shivering. They pushed me out of their sleeping bags and threatened me with horrible things if I ever told what happened.

They repeatedly called me "worthless." They told me they were going to tell all the kids at the school I would be attending in September what a loser I was.

I pulled my nearly naked body back into my own sleeping bag. I thought about collecting my gear and running out of the tent. But if I did, I would have to explain why I had left. The threats of my abusers rang in my head. Even if people believed me, they would see me as a filthy participant in a despicable act.

With my body in pain, and my heart heavy under an overwhelming sense of guilt, I sobbed. The other two boys slept soundly.

I heard the other scouts laughing and talking in nearby tents. I lifted the flap and saw the scout leaders sitting under a canopy with a lantern, engaged in a card game. My sense of loneliness was overwhelming.

Chapter 3

JUNIOR/SENIOR HIGH SCHOOL YEARS

The Continued Actions of My Abusers

Seventh grade was a difficult year for me in many ways. First, I found that I had been placed in what was called section 7-2. Most of my closest friends were in section 7-1. The 7-1 section was the academic or most likely college-bound students. I had always been in the top groups in elementary school and now found myself placed elsewhere. I later found out that the placement was based on performance on the sixth grade achievement tests. I didn't know that and the placement only reinforced my new negative self-image. It seemed to me that I was not as good as people used to think and this was just the beginning of the proof. It also reinforced my sense of loneliness, since my best friends were in the other section.

The second area of difficulty for me was the realization that, in fact, my two abusers actually had told stories about me to other students. I didn't know what they had told, but I knew from the way others treated me, and statements that they made to me, that they had been told something very bad.

When I passed the two abusers in the hall they snickered and laughed and often said things like, "Hey! Worthless." Sometimes they would speak to one of their friends walking with them and point and laugh.

I vividly recall one of their friends trying to get past me in the hall one day. He pushed me aside and said, "Get out of my way you worthless piece of sh— !" Then he laughed and called me other obscene names. I knew he must have heard those words from the other two. I didn't believe I could tell anyone about this treatment because it might lead to having to tell what had happened to me, and I was sure that no one would believe my side of the story.

I was one of the naïve 7th graders. In spite of the sexual experiences that I had been involved in, I still didn't know "the facts of life" until near the end of that school year.

Therefore, when my abusers or their friends made lewd sexual comments to me, I didn't know what they were talking about and they seemed to know it. That seemed to be part of their fun at my expense.

They often pointed across the cafeteria at me and laughed and whispered to their friends. Sometimes I would find notes that had been slid through the vents in my locker. They always managed to include references to me as "worthless". That type of behavior continued until the older of the two graduated three years later.

My Emotional Reaction

All through 7th grade I struggled with trying to figure out where I belonged. I knew I didn't want to be like the two who used me for their own entertainment, but I didn't think I was good enough to fit in with the kids I really liked. Part of it may have been the typical 7th grade syndrome, when you realize you are now at the bottom of the heap looking up. But for me it was more than that. I didn't like myself very much because of what had happened to me on that campout a few months before. The realization that, at first, I had willingly participated in something that ultimately turned out very bad caused me great confusion. I constantly questioned myself as to why I would do such a thing. I thought I should have just fought my way out or screamed that night in the tent or just anything to stop it. But I didn't, and that made me question my own self-worth and even my own sexual orientation at times. I heard other boys tell jokes about the actions of people who they referred to as "queer." I knew that those behaviors were part of what I had done and what had been done to me on that fateful night and also during the year when I was five years old.

Overall, I was very confused, and it seemed as though many people knew something horrible about me, thanks to my abusers telling stories. I also knew that whatever they were telling would not be something that cast them in a negative light. I thought they must be telling other kids lies about me as if they had no part in it themselves. I felt deep shame, but most of all fear and loneliness. I feared they would physically hurt me or someone in my family, as they had threatened that they would. I also feared that my friends and family would hear the lies they were telling and that the humiliation would be more than I could bear. I knew my parents would be devastated, humiliated, and terribly disappointed in me if they heard the lies.

My Search for God

All through elementary school I had willingly attended church and Sunday school, either at my parents' church or the church of close friends. My parents were members of the Presbyterian Church and were quite faithful in attendance and served in various offices. I was always willing to attend and sang in the choir and enjoyed Sunday school and Vacation Bible School. At least three times I attended week-long summer camps as part of the youth program of the Presbyterian Church.

There was a period of time when I was perhaps eight to ten years old that my parents stopped going to church and I went to a local Baptist church at the invitation of a neighbor and friend. During that period, I earned three years of perfect attendance pins for Sunday school and sang in the choir there.

The combination of training that I received in these two churches gave me an excellent foundation for the Christian faith. I had a love for God and believed the Bible was true from cover to cover. One time at the close of the Sunday school class at the Baptist church, I repeated the teacher's prayer to receive Christ as my personal savior, but I am not sure that I actually understood what I had done. Soon after that my parents started attending the Presbyterian Church again so I never had any follow-up counseling. In the Presbyterian Church I attended there was never any mention of personal salvation.

As a junior high student living in a world of emotional turmoil, I wondered how the God I loved could be allowing me to suffer so much. I thought that either He was angry with me because of my sin or I must be in the wrong church. In my small home town of four hundred people there were five churches, all of which professed to believe in the same God. However, they had vastly different methods of worship. I couldn't believe they could all be right. I began to ask adults questions and was surprised that few had any answers about why there were so many different churches. I even read in the encyclopedia about each of the denominations in our town in an effort to find the truth. We had the Presbyterian, United Methodist, Episcopalian, American Baptist, Independent Baptist, and Catholic churches from which to choose. No amount of reading gave me the answer I was looking for.

I continued to attend the Presbyterian Church and was generally satisfied with what I heard, but still felt that God was not pleased with me. I concluded that it was true that

God loved me, but that He didn't want to be close to me because of my past secret sin. I thought that if I could ever confess it openly and publicly that He would embrace me, but the thought of ever doing that was a hurdle too high for me. I viewed Him as a distant overseer in my life.

Confused about whether I would go to heaven when I died, I asked my mother and my Sunday school teacher who both assured me that I didn't have to worry about that as long as I believed in God. One person told me that unless I had committed some horrible sin, I would definitely go to heaven. I was convinced that I had committed a horrible sin, and since I had, my conclusion was that God couldn't love me. Nevertheless, I continued to seek an answer I could live with. If I had committed a sin God could not forgive, what was the use of living, unless it was just to prolong the hell that would surely follow my death. These thoughts lingered in my mind for most of my junior and senior high school years.

The Life-Changing Bus Ride

In the ninth grade, I was allowed to be on the junior varsity basketball team. I say allowed because there is no way I was good enough to play on a regular basis. I tried out and was cut from the squad, but later was asked to join the team when someone got hurt. I probably provided some assistance in practice as the opponent for the really good players to play against. I seldom got to play in the real games, except to give someone a rest or if the coach, in an act of compassion, put me in with ten seconds to play. In that respect, I was a pretty good bench warmer.

One night, after an away game where our team lost in a very close match with one of the best teams in the league, I was sitting alone on the bus just staring out the window when the coach got on the bus and came back and sat with me. He apologized for not putting me in the game that night. I immediately told him that I totally understood and that he did the right thing. I wouldn't want to have been responsible in any way for our team losing the game. He asked, "Then you're not upset about not playing tonight?" I replied, "No, I don't need any more pressure."

He told me that he noticed that I often didn't "hang out" with the other guys and overall didn't seem very happy much of the time. I sat up and paid attention to that statement. I couldn't believe that anyone had made that observation, particularly a teacher and coach. Of course, I denied that anything was wrong and assured him that I was just fine.

He asked me what type of things I was thinking about doing after high school graduation. I had to admit that I didn't have much direction at that point. The only thing I had thought about was working on the family farm or working in one of the local industries operating some sort of machine.

He began to question me about whether I had thought about going to college. I told him that no one in my family had gone to college and that I didn't see that as an option for me either. He pursued the point and finally stated that he thought I should definitely consider college. I told him that I didn't think I was smart enough. His reaction to my statement was one of great encouragement to me. He told me that he, too, had never thought of college when he was my age. He had considered a career in the military. He hadn't thought of himself as the college type of student. I could certainly relate to that. I asked him what changed his mind and his reply became the beginning of a life-changing experience for me.

He told me that he had a high school teacher who took a real interest in him and became an encourager and cheerleader for him. He said it was that person's confidence, support, and encouragement, which started him on the path that led him to where he was that night. Then, he told me that he had that kind of confidence in me as well. He mentioned the names of several of the most successful and popular upperclassmen at our school. He asked what I thought about those people and I responded that I was impressed, but that I could never achieve like they had done. Again, he questioned me. He asked, "Why do you have such a low opinion of yourself?" I replied, "It's just the facts and there is nothing I can do about it." He said, "No, I refuse to accept that and you should reject that kind of thinking too." He said that I could do anything I wanted if I worked hard and put my mind to it.

He encouraged me to study harder and make a sincere effort to always get the best grades possible. He told me that, if I really wanted to get the most out of my school experience, I should get involved in clubs and school functions as much as possible. He said I needed to "take charge" of my school years and not just coast along and miss out on some of the best years of my life.

As the bus pulled into our school, he stood up, placed his hand on my shoulder and said "I'm going to be watching you and I expect to see some changes in the days ahead. You can definitely do it!" I expressed my appreciation for the fact that he took the time to talk to me, but words could not express the significance that his attention and interest in me meant in the process of turning me around and changing my course of action over the next several years.

High School: A Breath of Fresh Air

My high school years were like a breath of fresh air in comparison to the junior high days. I was invigorated by the encouragement given by my coach the previous year. The oldest one of my abusers had graduated the previous June and I felt great relief knowing he was not around every day. I did enroll in all academic classes and began tenth grade with a burst of enthusiasm. The coach was one of my teachers that year and he continued to encourage and challenge me. Sometimes as I was walking out of his classroom he would say, "Don't forget, I'm watching you." Other times, if I walked past his classroom between classes and he happened to be standing in his doorway, he would look at me and point a finger and smile. I interpreted it as a sign that he was watching and I was encouraged.

I had spent hours that summer between ninth and tenth grade considering what type of career I would choose if I went to college. I would go to my room and turn on music and lie on the bed and stare at the ceiling. I was continually fixed on the idea that I would like to do something where I could help children who, like me, had been victims of sexual abuse. However, I didn't know how to explain that to anyone without disclosing my own abuse and that was definitely out of the question.

My Guidance Counselor

I discussed with some adult friends the idea of my desire to help children who had problems, and they steered me in the direction of the psychology field. I began to read about psychology and decided that it might be the career I was looking to pursue. I went to our school guidance office to discuss the idea with a guidance counselor. I wanted to be sure that I was taking the right courses for that field and to check out whether there were any local colleges that taught psychology as a major.

When I met with the guidance counselor, I was substantially knocked backward in my newfound self-confidence. When I told him my interest he said, "What's the matter, you too good to be a farmer like your father?" I reminded him that I was the third-born son in the family and that our farm wasn't big enough to support all of us. He further informed me that he didn't think I was college material and that at that point my grades were not good enough to get me into any college.

I don't know whether my guidance counselor was serious about those comments or whether he was just trying to get me motivated to do better. It may be that it was a little of both. I can view it that way now, but I certainly didn't see that possibility then. I was devastated by his comments. I thought I was back to square one as far as my self-confidence and motivation were concerned.

I decided to not let those comments go without telling my coach/teacher. One morning on my way to my homeroom, I stopped by his classroom and told him what the guidance counselor had said. He was visibly angered. He said that the guidance counselor didn't know me as well as he did and I should keep working to prove the counselor wrong. At that point, my trust in my teacher was so great that I decided to take his advice and actually did work even harder. He again assured me that I could make it in college.

My Best Friend

In addition to the support I received from my teacher I was also strongly supported by one of my best friends, Matt Orkins, who was an outstanding student. He was well-known for being one of the best students in our class. His friendship toward me gave me confidence at the time I needed it most. However, I never had the courage to tell even him about my abuse and its effects on me. I think I was afraid that somehow he would think less of me, although now I know that would not have been the case.

We had similar backgrounds in that both of our fathers raised thousands of chickens and we both worked for our fathers every day. Whenever I ran into an academic problem, especially in the mathematics areas, I could always count on Matt to be there to assist me. He never made me feel stupid; in fact, the opposite was the case. He often pointed out areas where he thought I was more capable than he. We often spent time together outside of school as well. We both enjoyed classical or, at least, very conservative music. Sometimes we would go to a public library and browse for books [and girls of course]. Our tastes in music were quite different from most teenagers. At the local restaurant in my home town the owner told me that she could always tell I was there when she heard the jukebox playing. She said most teens didn't play that kind of music.

We were both serious minded and were often told that we seemed much older than our actual ages. However, we did like to joke around too. One female classmate was not impressed with our humor and once said that we were "simple minded and easily amused." We have never forgotten that statement and have come to be proud of it and joke about it to this day.

During the summer between our junior and senior years, when we were both seventeen, Matt and I traveled by bus from Elmira, New York to New York City and stayed in his aunt's and uncle's apartment while they were out of town. We were the typical tourists visiting sites such as the Empire State Building, Statue of Liberty, the United Nations, Rockefeller Center, the Bronx Zoo and Radio City Music Hall. Matt had done all of this before, but it was all new to me. I couldn't believe the lights on Broadway and the maze of subway tunnels. From New York we traveled by train to Lake Champlain to spend a few more days with another relative of Matt's. Then we took a bus back home. The trip was quite an experience for a couple of farm boys from the hills of Pennsylvania. I still cannot believe that my parents allowed me to take such a trip without any adult chaperone. I think it proves how mature people thought us to be for our ages. That trip did wonders for my confidence since I didn't know any other seventeen year olds who had done such a thing. Teachers and students alike seemed impressed about our adventure.

My Late Blooming

My sophomore, junior and senior years of high school were definitely periods of late blooming for me. I had a new burst of determination and a sense of freedom that I had not had in the junior high years. The encouragement of my friend, Matt, and my teacher was like adding jet fuel to my whole being. I discovered that I was able to achieve academically again, and I actually volunteered to get involved in extra-curricular activities. By the end of tenth grade, I had been chosen to be a member of the National Honor Society and had become an outgoing member of our class. Ultimately, by the end of high school I had been elected as class president, president of the National Honor Society and president of the Student Council.

I had a great opportunity to test my leadership skills in high school and received much praise and recognition from the teachers and school administrators. With every successful endeavor I gained more confidence and became more determined to prove that I was not worthless. I remember one teacher telling me that she was very proud of me and that she had always believed that I could excel in school. I had always thought that, too, until that fateful summer night when I was twelve, when the phrase, "worthless," was seemingly branded into my brain.

Lingering Negative Thoughts

In the midst of all the successes that I had during those high school years, I never lost the lingering thoughts about being worthless and the concern that, at any time, my little secret about what had happened when I was twelve would be known and I would be humiliated. I had learned to become a very good actor and appeared outwardly to be happy and content. Inwardly, I was always concerned that I would fail at what I was expected to do. It was a great honor to be in the offices that I held, but with those offices came responsibilities which I often believed I was ill equipped to handle. I thought that the only reason I was given the opportunity to fill those positions was because of what people thought about me based on the façade that I hid behind every day.

In my mind, I was not the person most people thought me to be. I felt like I was living a lie. Sometimes I escaped to my bedroom and sulked, trying to imagine what I would do if I failed. My ultimate conclusion each time was that I could not allow failure. That would prove my worthlessness, and I couldn't accept that possibility. Those days were the beginnings of my thoughts that everything I did had to be as perfect as I could make it.

Overwhelming Migraine Headaches

During high school I started having migraine headaches regularly. They were what doctors today describe as complex migraines. They always started with an aura, including numbness in my hand, face and tongue along with visual distortions. Then, they progressed to nausea and pain in my temples and deep in my eye sockets. The pain would become so severe that it caused vomiting. This condition usually lasted from twelve hours to two days or more. During that time I was extra sensitive to light and sound. Once the pain subsided I would sleep for most of the next day.

During my senior year, I had an unusual experience with the migraines. One day I felt the aura coming on while sitting in a class. The teacher was aware of my tendency to have migraines and I had permission to get up, walk out and go to the nurse's office any time I felt I needed to do so. I got up and walked out into the hallway and the visual distortions were so great that I couldn't find my way around. Someone saw me and recognized that something was wrong. I asked for assistance in getting to the nurses' office. My mother was called and I went home. Later that day I was admitted to the hospital for observation and testing.

An odd thing happened that night in the hospital. I recall getting out of bed in the night to go to the bathroom. I was later told that a nurse came in and found me unresponsive, lying on the floor halfway to the bathroom. I have vague recollections of being back in bed and people around me. I was told that I did not respond to any commands from the doctor or nurses.

In the middle of the night I was transferred, by ambulance, to a larger hospital an hour away. I was taken to their psychiatric unit and put to bed. When I awoke a few hours later I was confused about where I was and how I had gotten there. When everything was explained to me I had only sketchy recollection of the events.

I was soon moved to another floor in the hospital and a series of tests began in an effort to determine the cause of my visual distortions and other unusual symptoms. I had a spinal tap and an electro-encephalogram. No problems were shown on those tests; however, it was discovered that a bone in the septum of my nose, which I had broken years earlier, was putting pressure on the optic nerves in my head. Later that year, while in my freshman year at college, I had surgery to correct that problem.

I remember sitting in our family doctor's office getting the report on all the testing that had been done. He acknowledged that the pressure on the optic nerve was likely a factor in the cause of the headaches. However, he also indicated that stress from external sources could also be a contributing factor. I knew that there was a lot of external stress just from my efforts to achieve at school. However, I also knew that there was much emotional stress that never seemed to go away. I never seemed to be able to relax and be satisfied that I had done enough to offset those feelings of "worthlessness."

I constantly viewed my efforts as being weighed on a set of scales. I thought I had to build up enough good things on the one side, so that if my secret ever became known, perhaps the good things I had done would outweigh the bad and all would not be lost. Whether consciously, or unconsciously, I don't know, but that seemed to be my mode of operation for the next several years of my life.

Chapter 4

TURNING POINTS

There were two more events that became major turning points for me during my senior year in high school. One was connecting with the young woman who would later become my wife, and the second was that I finally understood the spiritual mysteries that had been eluding me for the previous 5-6 years.

Meeting My Future Wife

Peggy and I had been in the same grade at our small Junior/Senior high school since seventh grade. However, we were always in different sections of that grade and, therefore, did not have classes together. I became well acquainted with her because we were both in band and there was a certain closeness among the band members. We particularly enjoyed the marching band all summer and the bus rides to and from those events.

One thing I knew about Peggy was that she came from, what my friends and I called, a "very religious family." Although I was interested in dating some of the girls in our class, I had not thought about dating Peggy, partly because we weren't together that much, and I had heard that her parents required a boy to meet with them before he could date any of their three daughters. That was certainly not something I would have been interested in or comfortable doing.

During October of our senior year, both Peggy and I had the privilege of being chosen to participate in the county band event. It was an all-day Saturday activity with a concert in the evening. The band members were representatives from all the county school districts.

During the lunch break that day, I sat beside Peggy and we began to talk. I don't remember what the topic of our conversation was, but I know she impressed me. I had a totally different view of her. I don't think that before that day we had ever carried on much of a conversation. I certainly didn't view her as some religious fanatic, but rather a very nice person who I would like to get to know better. I knew that she was well thought of by the teachers and was also in the National Honor Society, of which I was the president.

I also remembered that during our junior year the teachers had selected me to represent our school at Keystone Boys' State while she had been selected to be the school's representative at Keystone Girls' State. These were programs whereby a student spent one week in residence at college learning about state and local government through a participatory process.

After that day was over I continued to think about our conversations and definitely wanted to have more of them. I decided to "bite the bullet" and take the risk of having to meet with her parents before going on a date with her. I asked Peggy to accompany me to the high school all-star basketball game at a local college. She responded by saying, "I'll have to ask my parents," just as I had expected. To my great surprise she came back to school the next day and said they told her she could go. There would be no meeting ahead of time with her parents. She said, "My parents feel that they already know you through many of the school activities." Additionally, Peggy's father and my father had both served on the school board together for approximately twenty years and were well acquainted.

We went to the game and shocked our classmates as we walked in together. I remember a good friend leaned over and asked me quietly, "Is this like a date or something?" I responded by saying, "Yeah, something, we'll see how it goes." I never went on a date with another girl after that night.

The Beginning of My Spiritual Enlightenment

On the way to the game that first night Peggy gently mentioned some things about her family and her church activities. I don't think it was an intentional attempt to influence me, but rather just so much a part of who she was that it became a normal part of the conversation. I was genuinely interested in her family and also what it was that gave them that label of "very religious." I quickly discovered that she was a Baptist and that her grandfather was a Baptist minister. I could immediately relate to her beliefs since I had attended a Baptist church and earned three years of perfect attendance pins in that Sunday school. Of course, six or seven more years had passed since that time.

After I brought her home from the game I asked if we could go out again soon. She suggested that I just come over and spend time with her at her house the next weekend.

That sounded great and much cheaper as well. When that night came it didn't take long before we were talking about the church again. Her dad came in from doing barn chores and he and Peggy's mother sat and talked with me in the living room. I figured that was the equivalent of the pre-date meeting I had heard about. They were wonderful people who put me at ease immediately. I recall her dad saying, "So, I hear you're almost a Baptist." I squinted, questioning what he meant. Then he said, "Peggy says you went to the Baptist church in Tioga for three years." I confirmed that I had and realized that it would be good if I suggested that it was a good experience. Her mother fed me well with ice cream and cake and thus ended my "interview" with them.

It was a couple of weeks later that Peggy and I had another date where we went out. As we traveled, I told Peggy that I wanted to talk about what she believed about God, the Bible and Jesus. She was more than willing. It was like she was just waiting for the opportunity. She began to talk about "salvation" and being "saved." These were not totally foreign to me since I had heard them at the other Baptist church. I showed my nervousness by saying that, "The only time I had ever heard the word salvation was when it had the word army after it." We laughed and then she went on to explain what those words meant to her.

Serious Spiritual Discussions

I'll state this as it came across to me at that point in my life. Peggy explained that the Bible says that every one of us has sinned and fallen short of what God expects of us. That was reassuring to me, since I certainly believed that I had failed God in my actions. She went on to explain that we all deserve to go to hell as punishment for our failures, but that God provided a way for us to escape the punishment we deserved. She said that God loved us so much that he sent Jesus, his only son into the world to die on the cross and take our punishment. She went on to say that if we believed in God and Jesus and what he had done for us on that cross we could be sure that God would forgive our sins and we could be sure of going to heaven.

I assured Peggy that I had heard all of that information before and that I did believe it. Those facts were taught in the Presbyterian Church where I had grown up and also in the Baptist church I had attended for three years. I remember quoting *John 3:16*, "*For God so loved the world, that he gave his only begotten Son, that whosoever believeth in Him should not perish, but have everlasting life.*" I knew that I did believe that those points were true, but in my mind I could not understand why I still felt guilty, dirty and worthless. And, I still felt that God was not someone close to me, but rather, a wonderful, loving super power somewhere out there, distant from people. Nonetheless, I loved this conversation with Peggy because I had a yearning to know more about God.

Later that evening when we returned to Peggy's house she gave me some little pamphlets that she called gospel tracts and asked me to read them over. When I asked if we could go out again the following weekend she suggested that I just come over to her house and watch television, listen to music and possibly talk some about the information in the pamphlets she had just given me. Again, I thought that was a great and inexpensive way to have a date. I had never done that with any other girl I had dated.

The next weekend came and I was delighted to spend time at Peggy's house again. Her parents were again there and the food her mother brought out was fantastic. Peggy asked if I had read the pamphlets, or tracts, as she called them, which she had given to me the previous weekend. I had to admit that I had only glanced at them and hadn't seriously looked at them so I could discuss the contents. Before going to bed, Peggy's mother gave me a small thirty page booklet. She told me that Peggy had told her that I had a lot of questions and that this booklet was a set of questions with answers that I might find useful. I was happy to receive it.

I read that little booklet from Peggy's mother and the smaller tracts that Peggy had given me before I went to sleep that night. Again, they reinforced everything that Peggy had already told me, but in more detail. They each included a model prayer that included what one was supposed to say if he or she believed what was included there and wanted to be sure of going to heaven. If a person did that, then he was supposed to be able to know that he was "saved." I read and I prayed those prayers, but honestly, I still wasn't sure it had made any difference in my eternal destiny.

Finally, I Understood

As the weeks passed I continued to spend time with Peggy and her family every Friday or Saturday night. I eventually started going to her house on Sunday afternoons and attended the evening service at her Baptist church. Soon I was going for dinner on Sundays, after I had attended church with my own parents. All this was in the spring of our senior year of high school and our relationship was growing stronger every week.

As I look back over the events of those days I can see how the Lord was working at every turn. The pastor of Peggy's church was preaching through the book of Romans during those Sunday nights. He gave the clearest presentation of the gospel message that I had ever heard, at least since I was old enough to comprehend it.

Romans is a book of the Bible that contains all the verses a person needs to understand how to be saved and assured of heaven after he dies. It clearly demonstrates God's love for mankind in a way that I had not understood. I listened intently each week as the message slowly began to settle into my brain and I was able to assimilate it with other teachings I had received, either through reading, or the conversations with Peggy and her parents. I still have notes that I took during those messages and I often refer back to them.

The Message I Heard

This is the message the pastor presented during those evening services. Romans 3:23 states that, "*For all have sinned, and come short of the glory of God.*" This was totally compatible with what Peggy had shared with me weeks earlier. However, this time I realized that it wasn't just my actions alone that made me a sinner, as I had thought, but ever since the sin of Adam and Eve, we are all born sinners. We are born with a sin nature that separates us from God. Therefore, every person is bound for hell when he is born, just by the fact that he is a descendant of the first parents, Adam and Eve.

In Romans 6:23 God says, "*For the wages of sin is death; but the gift of God is eternal life through Jesus Christ our Lord.*" Once again, I believed that I deserved death for the sins I knew I had committed. But I had a new realization; I was not alone in deserving that destiny. God had said that even the best people I could think of would suffer that same fate. Fortunately, that was not the end of that pronouncement from God. He said that God had provided a gift through Jesus Christ and that gift was eternal life. The question I had to ask myself now was, "How can I be sure to get that gift?" I still didn't feel as though I deserved it.

In the weeks that followed, I thought the pastor must have been reading my mind because the next verses he shared were Ephesians 2:8 and 9. These verses state, "*For by grace are ye saved through faith; and that not of yourselves: it is the gift of God: Not of works, lest any man should boast.*" It was clear to me that none of us deserve God's free gift of salvation from an eternity in hell. We cannot earn it or be "good enough" to deserve it. It was by God's grace and love that he provided for our redemption from that fate. If we could earn it or be "good enough," then God would not get the glory, but rather we would get the praise for our behavior. Besides, how could a person measure what is "good enough" for God. How would you be able to go through life not knowing whether or not you had measured up to God's standard?

The message from God in Romans 5:8 was clear. It states, "*But God commended His love toward us, in that, while we were yet sinners, Christ died for us.*" I began to realize that it wasn't a matter of whether I, or anyone else, deserved God's gift of eternal life. God had provided that gift for me while I was a sinner. It wasn't even possible to be "good enough" to deserve the gift of eternal life. There was no way to earn the gift through our own efforts. God loves us so much that He provided a way for us to be redeemed from our position as sinners. However, we have to consciously accept that gift.

I understood that it wasn't just the sins that I knew I had committed that would cause me to deserve hell, but also the sin nature with which I had been born. Now I understood more fully that I was a sinner and that my sin would send me to hell, except for the fact that God had already provided the remedy for that problem by sending Jesus into the world. It wasn't just that Jesus had come into the world that was significant. It was the reason He came and what He did that was the main point. Jesus came to take the penalty that I deserved and pay the price that had to be paid for sin. That price was the shedding of innocent blood, blood that came from someone who wasn't a sinner. That was the only sacrifice acceptable to God and Jesus was the only one who could give it.

I finally realized the full meaning of concepts I had learned in my earlier years in church and Sunday school classes. I knew that back in the Old Testament God had established the practice of sacrificing a lamb, without blemish, for the people to have their sins forgiven. It was the shedding of that animal's blood that met God's requirement for forgiveness.

Now I was able to see that the sacrificial lamb was a perfect picture of what was to come when God provided His Son, Jesus, like a spotless lamb, to shed His blood on the cross in order for people to have their sins forgiven. The prophet Isaiah proclaimed in chapter 53 verses 4 through 6: *"Surely He hath borne our griefs, and carried our sorrows: Yet we did esteem Him stricken, smitten of God, and afflicted.*

But He was wounded for our transgressions; He was bruised for our iniquities: the chastisement of our peace was upon Him; and with His stripes we are healed. All we like sheep have gone astray; we have turned every one to his own way; and the Lord hath laid on Him the iniquity of us all."

Next, I understood that simply knowing about Jesus and his sacrificial death on the cross as payment for sin was not the end of God's plan. I recall hearing the pastor clearly report that even Satan believes in Jesus and knows that He died on the cross to pay for the sins of people. He said it wasn't knowledge of the facts that would assure me of heaven; it was the realization that I was a sinner who could not save myself from hell. I had to confess my sinful state to God, ask for his forgiveness and profess my faith in Jesus as my only savior, and accept that free gift of salvation. In 1 John 1:9 it says, *"If we confess our sins He is faithful and just to forgive us our sins, and to cleanse us from all unrighteousness."*

As the pastor concluded the evening service each night he prayed and asked, "Is there anyone here who has never made that decision to accept that free gift of salvation?" Everyone had their heads bowed, and he asked that if anyone wanted to make that decision that night to just raise their hand. I knew I had not made that decision yet, but I never raised my hand.

One night after I returned home I could not get the pastor's words out of my mind. I did believe everything he had preached and everything that Peggy and her parents had shared with me about how to be sure of eternal life in heaven. I knelt down beside my bed and prayed. I confessed that I knew I was a sinner and that I was bound for hell. I asked God to forgive me of all my sins and professed to him that I accepted the gift of salvation that he provided through the shed blood of Jesus. Furthermore, I asked him to help me live free from the guilt and depression that had been such an integral part of my life for years. After that, I crawled in bed, and I believe I fell asleep that night with peace in my heart and a smile on my face.

Life Was Sweet

I could not wait to get to school the next morning to see Peggy and tell her that I had prayed to accept Jesus as my savior. I am not sure if I told her face to face or slipped her a note, but I remember that when we did meet after she found out she seemed overjoyed. That weekend when I arrived at Peggy's house and entered through the back door, her mother met me and hugged me and said tearfully, "I'm so happy to hear the good news. We have been praying for you for weeks."

As I think back on it, I had only been dating Peggy for 3 or 4 months at that point. So much had happened in that short timeframe. Our relationship had deepened in so many ways. I knew that even if our relationship with each other didn't last, no one could take away my new-found relationship with the Lord. However, our relationship did last and our love for one another continued to grow. Likewise, my relationship with the Lord continued to develop.

I was eager to talk about my newfound faith and understanding of God's word. The first person I shared it with was my mother. I found out that she also believed the same as I, had been baptized in the local river, as a child, and was a member of the Baptist church in our town before marrying my father. Next, I shared with my sister who is nearly 9 years younger than I. She seemed to understand all the principles I explained and ultimately prayed the same type of prayer that I prayed to accept Christ as her savior. There were others who I shared my faith with who were less open to receive what I had to say.

Needless to say, I was elated most of the time. Peggy and I continued to develop our relationship after we graduated from high school that spring. I lived at home and commuted to Mansfield State College to be trained to teach Special Education, while she took a job with New York Telephone Company and also lived at home. For the next three years I continued to attend the Baptist church with Peggy and her family. Since I was in college and needed something typed nearly every week, I soon established a habit of going to her house on Tuesday nights for her to type for me, as well as on the weekends. It was much more fun than learning to type myself at that point.

During those years in college, life was truly sweet. It was an experience I enjoyed and since I got to be with Peggy every week it was an ideal situation. I had the advantage of independence and yet living at home sheltered me from a lot of responsibilities other than my studies and a little farm work with my family. My newfound understanding of my spiritual condition was a relief from the guilt and shame I had experienced during my junior and senior high school years. I felt free and at peace with God and myself and lived life everyday with great expectations of good things to come.

I graduated from college in 1967 and Peggy and I were married that summer. The previous three years had been like a dream come true. We were married in her home Baptist church by her grandfather, assisted by a former pastor. We moved to another state where Peggy had an office job with a telephone company and I was hired to be a Special Education teacher.

Chapter 5

CHRISTIAN SERVICE EXPERIENCES

Matthew 5:16

"Let your light so shine before men that they may see your good works and glorify your Father which is in heaven."

I was very excited to know that I had the assurance of an eternity in heaven with Jesus. I was eager to live in a way that would be evident to everyone I met that Jesus was the priority in my life. The first year of our marriage we lived in an unfamiliar, new area of the country, approximately twenty-five miles north of Baltimore, Maryland. At first we attended various small churches and tried to find one similar to the country church we had both become accustomed to at home. We did find some very friendly churches and one large one that we liked very much.

The year we moved to Maryland was the year that Martin Luther King was assassinated and racial riots broke out in many towns and cities of the state. Both of us were warned by people that we worked with that it was unsafe to go out in the country and take walks along country roads, something we loved doing back home. The racial tensions were so great that we were uncomfortable even going out in our car after dark. Peggy was accustomed to taking walks during her lunch break at her job in Elmira, New York, but her boss in Maryland told her that, under no circumstances, was it safe for her to do that where she worked there.

Neither of us had ever had any reason to be prejudiced and worked hard at staying unbiased in our new places of work and residence. After only about six months we decided that we did not want to live in that area on a long-term basis. I interviewed and was hired for a junior high Special Education teaching job in Horseheads, New York. We would be able to live back in our home area once again. In April, we were pleased to find out that we were going to be blessed with our first child the following November.

Once we knew we were going to be moving back home we stopped looking for a small church and settled into the large church where we were very happy. In some ways, we didn't want to be noticed so that people would want us to get more involved, since we knew we would be leaving soon.

In June of 1968, we moved back to Millerton, Pennsylvania. We had our mobile home, which we had purchased in Maryland, hauled up and Peggy's dad gave us a wooded lot on the edge of the farm on which to set it up. We could see the barns and her parents' house from our yard and yet we had privacy too. I have often been asked, "How could you stand to live so close to your in-laws?" I never had a problem answering that it was pure joy and nothing but a great advantage. I think Peggy's parents were more concerned about bothering us than anything else.

Back In Our Home Church

Worked with the Teens: We immediately started attending Peggy's home church and soon it was my home church as well. I was baptized by immersion in March of 1969, a requirement for church membership, and joined soon after. It was as if we had never been gone. Soon I was asked to teach the teen Sunday school class. At first we met in a very small room and the students were nearly sitting on each other's laps. However, a new addition was added to the church which gave the teens their own room. Many weeks there were fourteen to sixteen energetic students in attendance. It was a terrific learning experience for me to teach that class. Carefully following the teacher's guide each week, I know I learned as much or more than the students.

Shortly after starting to teach the Sunday school class Peggy and I were asked to begin a teen youth group. I think because we were young and energetic, we seemed to be the logical choice. We worked with the teens for the next twenty years.

During those twenty years we worked with the teens, we had Sunday night youth group meetings, prayer group on Wednesday evenings and, at least once per month, some sort of recreational activity. Many times we hosted the group at our house where we played games, enjoyed food, and I always had a devotional time as well. We traveled to Niagara Falls and Washington, D.C., and also held numerous campouts, scavenger hunts and various other activities.

Held Various Church Offices: Early in my church membership I was elected to the positions of Deacon and Trustee. It was an incredible privilege to hold those offices at such an early stage of my Christian life. A Deacon is to assist the pastor in the spiritual matters of the church, while a Trustee is responsible for the business affairs. I continued to hold one or both of those offices continuously for the next thirty years.

During those years there were times when issues arose that required the officers to mediate disputes between people in the congregation and the pastor. I always disliked those times. Often the positions that I had to take on issues led to either the people, or the pastor, being unhappy with me and other members of the deacon or trustee boards. It was during these times that I realized that my tendency to be a "people pleaser" once again came to light and added to my stress. Most situations could not be resolved so that people on both sides of an issue were equally satisfied.

The stressful times on one of those boards often led to my wanting to withdraw to protect myself from hurt. When people I loved became angry and disappointed with me, my natural tendency was to escape, or at least, to withdraw within myself. Unfortunately, that kind of behavior usually led to becoming depressed. It also reinforced the old ideas from my youth. The voice inside my head was saying, "You are still worthless. Sooner or later everyone will know it."

Taught Adult Sunday School: After teaching the teen Sunday school class for twenty years, I began teaching the adults during Sunday school. I was extremely honored to be asked, but still felt inadequate in comparison to some of the adults who were included in the class. It was certainly a challenge to prepare and teach every week. I had no problem holding the attention of the teens over the years, but I thought adults would be much more difficult. In many ways I was correct. They had just sat through a morning worship service and many were sleepy and hungry.

I studied long and hard each week and tried to choose topics that I thought would interest them. I knew that getting them involved in discussion was critical, but I often failed because I was so anxious to get through a whole lesson each week. I soon learned that it was better to take two- three weeks to get through a lesson, than to rush through with no discussion.

All totaled, between the teen and adult classes, I taught Sunday school for over thirty-five years. It was a great pleasure and honor. It was an excellent way to be sure that I was reading the Bible and studying every week. I wish everyone could have that privilege.

Conducted Group and Individual Bible Study: Another important way the Lord allowed me to be in His service was through conducting both individual and group Bible studies with men.

I met nearly every week for five years with one man for Bible study at our home. He had recently accepted Christ as his savior, but wanted desperately to learn and grow in his knowledge of the Bible. His sincerity sometimes put me to shame. He would occasionally phone our house during the day and ask Peggy to write down some questions that had come to his mind which he wanted to discuss with me that night. We became great friends and confidants.

Additionally, the Lord gave me the opportunity to teach part-time at Elmira College for twenty-six years, and on two occasions I conducted Bible studies in Elmira with students who I had met through my teaching there. Each Bible study lasted several weeks and, as always, was a growth experience for me as well as those who attended. On two occasions, the Lord allowed me to lead other men to accept Christ as their savior.

One of the groups I had been meeting with in Elmira had the habit of moving from place to place each week. There was one person in the group who was new to the Christianity concept and was always full of questions. He admitted that he was concerned whether he would go to heaven when he died. One particular week in winter, the study was to be held at his apartment. When I arrived he said, "No one else is coming because of the slippery roads, but you can come in if you want to." I believe that the Lord had all that planned.

That night he continued his questioning and I was able to show him, through God's word, how to be saved and sure of heaven. I asked him, "If you die tonight, where do you think you will go?" He admitted, "I'm pretty sure I would go to hell, because I've done some bad stuff in my day." I had flash backs of my own life before I accepted Christ. I shared my personal testimony and showed him the Bible verses that had been shown to me a few years earlier. He stated that he was truly sorrowful for his sin and that he knew he needed help. He indicated that he believed the Bible to be true and that he wanted to have Jesus forgive him. He prayed and accepted Christ right there in his apartment. We both cried tears of joy and hugged as I left.

When I got back to my car I used my cell phone to call Peggy, since I knew she would be concerned about the slippery roads. I told her, "You're not going to believe what just happened." I explained about my evening with great excitement. She, too, expressed joy and then said, "You be careful on those roads." I remember saying, "I don't care if I do wreck, it would be worth it considering what happened tonight." I did make it home safely, but realized that no matter how tired I am, the Lord blesses when I do His will.

The Effects of the Snare Continued

While I was in college, and the first couple of years of our marriage, I felt as though the grip that Satan had on me was gone. However, slowly but surely, as life got more complex, those old feelings of guilt, inferiority and low self-esteem started to invade my thoughts again.

During the last ten years before I was ensnared into a catastrophic experience with the Internet in 2001, Satan crept into my life and stole my joy of serving. It became increasingly more difficult for me to fulfill the jobs I had been given at church. I was still teaching the adult class and conducting Bible studies and was also the chairman of the church board. At the same time there were several stressful situations going on at my work as well. My old trait of trying to please everyone was again proving to be a major weight I felt I had to bear.

Peggy and I were informed by a new pastor of our church, that, as he went out calling on people in the community, he had heard some disturbing comments. He said that people told him that the reason that they didn't attend this church was because it was "run by the family on the hill." That was a direct reference to our family, meaning my mother-in-law and father in-law, Peggy's sister and brother-in-law, and Peggy and me.

Upon hearing that feedback I immediately wanted to resign from whatever offices I held and step back from all involvement other than attending. It was a crushing blow and the direct opposite of what I would have wanted the people of the community to feel. In no way did I want to be viewed as running anything at church, nor did I want to stand in the way of anyone else attending. The fact is that in the little country church, with a congregation that ranged over the years from twenty-five to seventy-five people, it was very difficult to find enough people who were willing to hold the offices. The majority only attended Sunday morning worship service and were satisfied with that level of involvement. There was Sunday school for all ages, including adults, Sunday evening services and Wednesday night prayer meeting. It is true that often Wednesday night's and Sunday evening's attendees were comprised mostly of our families. But we prayed that others would be more involved.

Once again, I wanted to resign my position and actually leave the church all together. Though I did not feel that I had done wrong, the pastor's statements made me question myself and my whole mental state. My first reaction was that when we went home that day I would never return. However, Peggy was adamant that we should not leave and several people from the congregation encouraged me to stay. We did stay; however, I am still not sure it was the right thing to do. I wanted to crawl into a cave somewhere and hide for a very long time.

Running in the Background

The above example is one of the most profound examples, but there were similar less devastating experiences over the years where our family was the source of criticism at church. Each time I heard it, my response was a strong desire to run away and escape or, at the very least, to withdraw from any active involvement. I suppose it was as though I was hearing those words "worthless" again. However, each time, Peggy was influential in convincing me to stay at what I was doing. Her whole family heritage was wrapped up in that little country church. Her great grandfather had been the head carpenter when it was built in the late 1800's. Her relatives had been among the founding members and her grandfather had been the pastor at one time. Her dad had been the son of that pastor. Her mother, who lived to be 87, had never attended any other church. Peggy had never attended any other church except for the brief ten months we lived in Maryland. I thought it would be selfish of me to take her away from the church she loved.

I am familiar with the concept of having computer programs "running in the background" while I am online or using other components of the computer. There are various purposes for these programs, but the point is that they monitor all your activity on the computer. Sometimes these monitoring programs can actually slow down the speed of a computer.

I believe that the influence of my negative childhood experiences was like the "program running in the background" of my mind. It was silent, but always there picking up on the thoughts and visual images that passed before me every day. Sometimes it condemned me and other times it lured me into destructive thoughts about myself. I had not been able to escape it after more than forty years. I suppose in reality it was my conscience at work influenced by the negative experiences, and, finally, by the lies that I came to believe about myself over the years.

Ambivalence Sets In

Events such as those at church and numerous situations I faced regularly at work caused me to become depressed. Eventually I began to feel distant from God. I knew that God had not left me, but I think I was frustrated over the circumstances surrounding me. I had the lingering sense that I didn't deserve to have the joy that God promised to those who love and follow Him. Soon I started neglecting regular Bible reading and prayer as part of my personal daily devotional time. I still prayed with Peggy everyday with rare exception, but it became more like a ritual to me.

At times I felt the presence of God very close to me, but at other times I held Him at "arms length" away from me. When conducting the Bible studies I was able to draw close to God and believe he guided me. When teaching the adult Sunday school class I studied diligently and sought His direction and frequently heard praise from members of the class. I poured everything I had into that teaching, so much so that it literally exhausted me afterword.

Many Sunday mornings after Sunday school I would say to Peggy, "Just get me home;" then I would sleep through the afternoon. I felt as though I had just been a performer on a stage and that what people saw was not the real me. I believed that I had just whipped up all the energy I could to put on a show to make people think that I was someone other than who I knew I was. I always appeared happy, joyful and friendly as a part of the mask I felt I had to wear to hide my true feelings about myself. I became quite proficient at faking it at church and other places.

Depression as Part of Me

After years of fluctuating between periods of ambivalence and fervency in my Christian walk, an overwhelming sense of depression surrounded me. The performing, as a method to hide my true feelings, became my way of life. Unfortunately, it never resolved anything. In fact, most likely it caused the depression to get stronger and stronger because I knew I was living a lie. I also felt that I was not living in the manner that God wanted me to live. Satan had a grip on me that dragged me down or, at least, slowed me down every day.

Vacations and weekends were no escapes from my feelings. I remember a time when Peggy and I were at our favorite camping place overlooking a lake. She enjoyed sleeping until eight o'clock, and reading and sunning herself while floating on a rubber raft. I enjoyed coasting along in our canoe or just sitting and staring at the lake while in deep thought. One time she came up behind me, placed her hands on my shoulders and asked, "What's wrong?" I responded, "Why do you think something is wrong?" She told me that I seemed sad or stressed about something. I, as usual, denied that anything was wrong and told her it was just my way of relaxing.

Peggy frequently reminded me that I needed to learn to enjoy being alone sometimes. She said, "You always want people around, but I like to be by myself much of the time." She was right. When we were camping I often sought out other campers to talk to or spend time with. At home I frequently wanted to invite friends over for dinner or just for an evening. Peggy is a great hostess and people seem to enjoy her hospitality. Many times she agreed and we did have people in, but she often repeated her question of, "Why can't you just enjoy being by ourselves more often?"

I had found that it was during those alone times that Satan beat up on me the most. Those were the times that I heard the condemning voices telling me how undeserving I was and what a hypocrite I was. There had been times when I sought the Lord during those attacks from Satan and found great victory. I would pray and read from the Bible and God would give me peace and rest. Unfortunately, there were more times when I tried to escape being alone or busied myself at some task to get my mind on something else.

I once heard that a definition of depression is that it is "anger turned inward." That seems like a good definition of the term as it relates to me. For years, I blamed myself for the abuse that happened to me when I was twelve. Then, I blamed myself for never having the nerve to tell anyone about it so that it could be dealt with appropriately. The guilt led to my endless effort at trying to cover up what I thought was my sin and my sense of worthlessness, as my abusers convinced me to believe.

I felt caught in a trap from which I could not free myself without exposing the awful truth that I did not want anyone to know. I don't know if I felt anger as much as frustration. There were definitely times when I wondered why God had allowed the abuse to happen to me. I loved Him and was thankful for His great provision for my salvation, but I also felt confused about why He had allowed me to be hurt.

Something inside of me said that I should not question God and I would not allow my thoughts to go there. However, I believe that is why I sometimes kept my relationship with God in that ambivalent status so that I would not have to deal with those thoughts. I could never bring myself to the point where I could be comfortable being angry with God. I recognized that He is all-powerful and all-knowing and I am insignificant in comparison. These are difficult concepts that I never figured out until I was well into my counseling later in life. I will discuss that in a later chapter.

Chapter 6

FORMAL EDUCATIONAL PURSUITS

Undergraduate Study

As I noted in an earlier chapter, I chose to live at home and commute to Mansfield State College for my undergraduate work. Initially, I planned to rent a room in a home in Mansfield and only come home on weekends. I thought that if I stayed at home I would be caught up in working on the farm and that would interfere with my studies. However, after one week I decided to move back home and give it a try. I found the hours of being alone very incompatible with my personality. I'm sure it would have been quite different if I had lived in one of the dormitories.

But, that additional expense seemed ridiculous considering that I only lived eight miles from the college.

My parents were very accommodating in fixing a great study place in my room at home. Also, we had a discussion about my need to be free from daily obligations on the farm in order for this arrangement to work out. It did work out and I ended up helping my dad on the farm a fair amount too.

During my years at Mansfield, Peggy and I continued to date and before my freshman year was over we had already decided that we wanted to marry and spend the rest of our lives together. Since she was already working I introduced the idea that perhaps I could get a part-time job and we could be married while I finished my degree. However, Peggy's wisdom won out and we decided to wait until I graduated.

I soon came up with another plan, though, that would hasten our plans for marriage. I learned that if I took extra credits each semester and attended summer sessions I could complete my four year degree in three years. Since I enjoyed college life, the extra hours studying were not a problem to me. I considered completing the courses to be my job and the key to unlocking the door to marriage sooner.

In July of 1967 I finished all of my course work for a Bachelor of Science Degree with a dual major of Special

Education and Elementary Education. I had miscalculated the dates for the summer school, so it worked out that, after Peggy and I were married on July 15th, I had to return to finish one more week of classes. My parents took that week as vacation and we lived at their house for that last week. I did the farm chores before and after classes while Peggy wrote thank you cards and packed for our move to Maryland for my first teaching position and her new job. I never attended a graduation ceremony at Mansfield because students who finished their requirements in the summer had to come back in January for a ceremony. Since we were living in Maryland, I opted out.

I never had many feelings of inadequacy during my years at Mansfield. I was successful in my coursework, and it was gratifying to prove to myself that I could do college level work and actually get better grades than I did in high school. Occasionally, I would recall the words of my guidance counselor who had told me he didn't think I was "college material." Then, I also recalled the teacher and coach who told me I could do anything I put my mind to. Overall, it was a great and enjoyable experience.

Graduate School

Master's Degree: Now that I had proven to myself that I was capable of successful college-level work I decided to pursue a Master's Degree from a reputable university. I was pleased to be accepted at Penn State to major in The Education of Exceptional Children. Since I was now teaching, my studies at Penn State had to be during the ten week summer sessions. It took three summers, along with a few night courses from Mansfield to transfer to Penn State, to complete that degree.

Once again, I was able to achieve Dean's list status which was gratifying and reassuring to me. I rented a room in a house in downtown State College since it was required that one be in residence for Penn State's Master's program. Old friends from high school lived a few houses down the street from where I roomed, and that helped with the loneliness issue that I had experienced my first week at Mansfield. Since I often had classes only three days per week I usually only stayed in the room a couple nights each week and then traveled back home.

Two of the three summers I was at Penn State Peggy was pregnant. The first summer she was due in November, and the third summer she was due in September. Due to the nearness of her delivery the third summer, I had to get special permission to miss the graduation ceremonies that were to be held at the end of the session.

My degree from Penn State assisted in opening the door for a better job almost immediately. I finished my coursework and started a new position within a week.

New York State Certification in School Administration and Supervision: Approximately eight years after my graduation from Mansfield, I decided to pursue New York State certification in School Administration and Supervision. I was working in New York State and often saw positions open that intrigued me, but they required this special certification. I discovered that a few people I knew were traveling about two hours away in the evenings to take courses at the State University of New York at Cortland, leading to the certification I was interested in.

I enrolled in the program and for the next two and a half years I drove or carpooled to Cortland for evening courses, until I had completed the required twenty-four credits. Once I had the certification, I was eligible for positions as a principal and/or education supervisor in a public school. Shortly after I received the certification, I was hired as a Special

Education Supervisor by our local Intermediate Unit or Board of Cooperative Educational Services.

The change in positions was a good move at the time and allowed me to work with a new base of school personnel, which would prove advantageous later as I moved on to the final position of my career. Each time I earned a new degree or certification, I became more confident in myself. However, soon after I was finished I started thinking about what I would do next because I never seemed satisfied that what I had achieved was sufficient.

Ph.D. in Human Service Administration: My last professional position was as the Executive Director of a human service organization. I soon discovered that there was much to learn in that field, and I began to pursue possibilities for acquiring a doctorate in Human Service Administration. I learned that most major university programs require that one be a full-time student in order to be admitted to their doctoral programs.

Eventually, however, I found a doctoral program that seemed perfect for my needs. That program was through Walden University, based in Minneapolis. First, I attended an informational meeting about the university in Rochester,

New York. What I heard there was exciting and I knew then that I wanted to pursue my degree through Walden. The doctoral program was accredited and included some of the most distinguished faculty from across the country.

I was required to attend an admissions workshop in Winston-Salem, North Carolina. Once again, I was not disappointed. I had to do a certain amount of writing and goal planning while there. At the close of the three-day workshop each participant was informed about whether he/she had been accepted. Fortunately, I was accepted. The thoroughness and quality of the material that was presented at the workshop was pleasing to me. I knew that, although not many people had heard about Walden at that point, I was going to receive a quality education.

Once I was accepted into the program, I was assigned an advisor. I was both pleased and somewhat intimidated by the person selected for me. She was the head of the Psychology Department at Boston University. She was the past president of the American Psychological Association and had served on the Board of the International Psychological Association. I was to be her one hundred and tenth doctoral advisee of her career. Wow! I wanted a quality education and I was sure I would get it with her guidance.

The Walden program required that students attend a minimum number of weekend seminars around the country. The faculty were also staff members on other college or university faculties. As I would attend the seminars it was possible to meet these faculty members and to select the ones who had the expertise that best suited my goals for the degree. I attended seminars in Philadelphia several times, as well as Washington, D.C., and Providence, Rhode Island. Additionally, I attended the required three-week intensive summer session in Minneapolis.

Due to the number of credit hours I had already accumulated prior to enrolling in Walden, I was able to complete my degree in two and half years while working full time. I can honestly say I enjoyed every minute of it. In fact, when I was finished I thought about getting another degree in another area of concentration.

I had the honor of being selected as the graduate whose dissertation most represented the goals of the university. Therefore, I was asked to give the graduate address during the ceremony in Minneapolis. It was a tremendous honor to stand before the other eighty-five graduates, the faculty and family members. Peggy, our two sons, and Peggy's parents flew with me to Minnesota for the event. It was my first college graduation ceremony and it was worth the wait.

One would think that this would finally be enough. It would seem as though after that achievement any thoughts of worthlessness would be gone forever. Oh, if it was only that easy. The jubilation was great for a few weeks and then Satan started planting his lies in my mind again. No, that wasn't good enough to make up for my worthlessness. I suppose I didn't really believe that lie, but I couldn't keep those thoughts from reappearing as soon as I faced some struggle or challenge at work.

Chapter 7

ATTEMPTS TO BREAK FREE THROUGH MY PROFESSIONAL PURSUITS

A career in Special Education would still allow me to work with children with special needs, which was the main reason I had wanted to be a psychologist. I was keenly aware of the struggles I had as a result of my abusive experiences of childhood and saw teaching special education students as a good way for me to work out some of my own issues. I have since learned that it isn't always a good idea to pursue a career for the purpose of trying to resolve your own past negative experiences. I have met many people who seemed to think they would be great counselors because they had been through so much counseling themselves. As I got to know them I often discovered that they still needed much more counseling and had a tough time sorting out their issues from those of their counselees. In fact, they often projected their own unresolved issues onto their clients. Hopefully, that did not become an issue for me as I was teaching.

Employment

Teaching Experience: As I noted earlier, in July of 1967, after I completed my Bachelor's degree, Peggy and I were married and then moved to Maryland where I taught primary age special education students. We soon learned that as a couple of farm kids from northern Pennsylvania, the suburban life twenty-five miles north of Baltimore was not for us. After one year we moved back home to Millerton, Pennsylvania and I taught junior high special education in the Horseheads, New York school district. During that time I had several students who not only had serious learning problems, but also had severe behavioral or emotional problems. I wanted to help those students, but felt so alone in the school because there was very little support available to help me deal with the behavioral problems. I had never been taught about the importance of involving the parents in the process of resolving student behavior problems. I was afraid that if I tried to contact parents about their child's behavior problems they would simply blame me and then I would feel incompetent and again, "worthless."

During the late spring of my second year of teaching in Horseheads, I made a wonderful discovery. One Friday afternoon as I was driving through Elmira, I noticed a large house with a sign on the front porch that read, "Children's House: Day Hospital Program, Elmira Psychiatric Center." After passing that place several times, I finally got the courage to stop to see if I could find out what services they provided there. I thought that if it was for children and it was part of a psychiatric hospital, I would be very interested in knowing if there was any possibility of a job there that I could do. As an undergraduate student at Mansfield we took field trips to a few State institutions for children and adults with mental retardation. I became interested in working with children in hospital or institutional settings because I wanted to work with those with severe problems, and they were usually found in the institutions during the 60's and 70's.

Around four o'clock on a Friday afternoon I stopped and went to the front door. I was shocked when I was greeted by a friendly man in his stocking feet who invited me to come in and sit down. I learned that this gentleman was Dr.

Robert West, [fictitious name] Director of the Children's Services provided there. No one else was there and I felt an immediate ease with this man as he explained what "The Children's House" was and the future plans for building a community-based Psychiatric Center on that site. Children's House was the beginning of what would become the children and adolescent units of the new Psychiatric Center. He explained that currently children from surrounding counties, who had either been hospitalized in state hospitals or who had been on home instruction due to severe behavioral problems in school, were attending a special educational and therapeutic program there at the house.

I explained to him about my teaching position and that I had been trying to teach severely emotionally disturbed students with very little support. He described all of the support services that were currently available at the Children's House and additional services that were planned as the Psychiatric Center developed. This was all music to my ears, of course. To be able to work with the type of students I wanted to work with and yet to be a part of team of professionals sounded too good to be true.

I finally got up the courage to ask the big question, "Are their going to be any teaching positions available soon?" He told me that he anticipated openings for the fall. I told him that I had one ten-week summer session left before earning a Master's degree in Education of Exceptional Children from Penn State University and that I would be very interested in applying for a position at The Children's House. He assured me that he would see that I got an application as soon as one was available.

True to his word, Dr. West had an Elmira City School District teaching application sent to me that summer. All the teaching staff would actually be Elmira City School District employees in this innovative collaborative program. All the other staff on the team would be employed by the Elmira Psychiatric Center. I completed the application, but was not interviewed and offered a position until approximately two weeks before school was to start. I accepted immediately and gave my resignation to the Horseheads School District. My supervisor there was very disappointed that I had not notified him sooner. However, I gave him the name of a friend of mine who was looking for a Special Education position. She was almost immediately hired and became an excellent fit for the class.

Elmira Psychiatric Center Experience: I began working at the Children's House the last week in August of 1970 as the Head Teacher for the elementary age children. That was the beginning of a wonderful experience. It was great to be in on the ground floor and be able to participate in the development of this innovative and creative program for severely emotionally disturbed children and adolescents. As it turned out, there had never been a community-based program like the one we developed anywhere in New York State and perhaps the whole country. It was considered to be a psycho-educational day treatment program where a team of mental health and education professionals worked with the children and their families to resolve their behavioral problems.

By 1972, the new buildings were finished and we were nearly ready to move from the house into our new quarters when a catastrophe happened. Our region received what was considered to be the flood of the century, and the new buildings, as well as our old house, were flooded up to the second floor. We were forced to find a temporary location for the next year while the new buildings were refurbished. That move was not as much of a problem as one might think because it gave us the opportunity to develop our services even more and add to our staff some wonderful additional team members before we would begin the inpatient component of our services.

A child psychiatrist was hired from California and he brought a particular approach to working with families that seemed to work well. He had written a book about his methods titled; *How to Get Your Children to Do What You Want Them to Do.*[1] The title alone was enough to attract a lot of attention. He began training all staff on how to use this approach in family therapy. No one was exempt from learning and using this technique. We all became family therapists, and families were required to participate if their children were enrolled in the program.

Soon after the psychiatrist was hired, a husband and wife team of social workers were hired. Both of them were also from California and were trained in the same family therapy technique that we had been taught by the psychiatrist. They immediately became the supervisors of all who were conducting the family therapy.

I was given opportunities and responsibilities in my employment at Elmira Psychiatric Center that I never would have had if I had stayed teaching in the school district. It was a tremendous growth experience and, for the most part, one that gave me a burst of confidence in myself. There were times, however, when people I supervised or worked with on the team gave me a lot of grief. I was only in my twenties, and it seems that some thought I was too young to be having the responsibilities that I had been given. I faced people who were borderline insubordinate at times, and that tested my confidence and self respect.

By 1975, I had another wonderful opportunity. I had taken the New York State Civil Service exam for a position titled Treatment Team Leader. It was required that a person had to be within the top three in scores in order to be hired. I was number four on the list when the position became available at Elmira Psychiatric Center. If I was hired for that position I would no longer be a school district employee, but rather an employee of the New York State Office of Mental Health.

There was a deadline whereby I had to be reachable on that list. None of the three above me were dropping out so I pursued the Team Leader position about fifty miles away at the Broome Developmental Center. That Center was for developmentally disabled individuals and was also a new small community-based facility, much like the Psychiatric Center. I was within the top three for that position. I thought the interview would be no more than two hours, but it was all day with several different people involved.

At the conclusion of the day I was excited about the possibility of working at the Developmental Center. I was confident that I could do the job and the people I met were magnificent. The main problem was, that since we had no intention of moving away from the new home we had built on the edge of Peggy's parent's farm, I would have to drive over an hour one way, twice a day if I took that job. A few days later I received a call offering me the position. I requested a couple more days before making my decision because there was still the possibility that one of the people who placed higher than I on the Elmira list might take another position and, therefore, make it possible for me to stay at the Psychiatric Center. On the last possible day, I was called to the personnel office. I assumed I was about to be told that it was clear that someone else would be offered the Elmira position. Much to my surprise, however, I was informed that, in fact, someone above me on the list had dropped out and I could now be hired.

It was a relief to find out that I could have the new position in Elmira, but now I had to make the sad phone call to the Unit Chief at Broome Developmental and turn down that position. We expressed appreciation to each other and he encouraged me to keep in touch in case I should ever change my mind. That whole experience was very gratifying to me. Just the fact that I was wanted in two places for very good jobs was like a dream come true. It did wonders again for my self esteem and eroded away some of those troubling thoughts of "worthlessness."

As the Treatment Team Leader, I was responsible to supervise all the members of the treatment team. I had to ensure that proper treatment planning was done and carried out. Additionally, I was to make sure we followed all the Mental Health regulations regarding the operation of a Day Treatment program. Again, I was sometimes challenged by staff who thought they knew better ways to do my job, but I always had tremendous support from my boss, Dr. West. I was occasionally caught in the middle when staff disagreed with decisions Dr. West had made, but rather than going to him they came to me and expected me to approach him. I always referred staff directly to him, but they seldom went.

During the late seventies, a new law was passed that mandated that all students with disabilities had to be educated in the least restrictive setting. We began to establish classes in the regular public schools with Elmira Psychiatric

Center staff assisting by working in the classrooms rather than staying at the Center. This approach won our program an award from the New York State Office of Mental Health as the most innovative service for emotionally disturbed children for that year.

In spite of my wonderful experiences in the job at the Psychiatric Center, I became anxious to move on to broaden my background even more. Whether it was the right thing to do, I do not know for sure. I know that it made Peggy quite nervous since the position I was seeking was initially only ten months per year; however, there was the promise that it would eventually go to eleven and then twelve months in a couple of years. I had prayed about it and felt confident in my decision.

Special Education Supervisor: Board of Cooperative Educational Services [BOCES] In 1978, I left the position at Elmira Psychiatric Center to accept a position as a Special Education Supervisor with BOCES. BOCES was considered to be an Intermediate Unit, whereby local school districts could contract with BOCES for specialized services when they did not have enough students with special needs to operate the services themselves. Seven school districts were involved with this particular BOCES. In my position, I had the opportunity to supervise all the different types of special education classes at some point, including emotionally disturbed, deaf, learning disabled, mentally retarded, physically handicapped and visually impaired.

The classes were all located in the regular public schools and that environment was appealing to me. Earlier I mentioned that I had wanted to work in an institutional setting with children with severe impairments. However, after eight years I was anxious to go back to the public school setting. Additionally, since the new Federal law mandated that all children with disabilities be educated in the least restrictive setting, that meant that even the severely disabled were now in the public schools.

During my seven years as a Special Education Supervisor, one of my greatest joys was the two years that I served as the building principal of a special school for emotionally disturbed children and classes for students with moderate to severe mental retardation. The classes for the emotionally disturbed children included the continuation of therapy support staff from Elmira Psychiatric Center. Therefore, my work was similar to what I did when I was at the Psychiatric

Center except that now I was working for the educational component of the program.

Loss of my Father

In August, 1984, my world was rocked when my father had a severe stroke and passed away. In the days and weeks that followed I became depressed and felt like a ship drifting aimlessly at sea. I sat in my office many days staring out the window and thinking about my father and the wonderful memories I had of him. I knew that he was proud of me and all the education and various jobs I had held. I was the first one of our family to go to college and he was very pleased. I once talked with a friend from my hometown of Tioga, Pennsylvania, who told me that to listen to my dad talk one would think that I was the state governor at the very least.

For several weeks after losing my dad, I felt as though I had lost my focus both in my career and personal life. I lost my satisfaction with my current job and began to concentrate on what else might lie ahead for me.

I never seemed to lose my desire to continuously advance in my professional field. I think it was all a part of my quest to prove my worth. It became clear that the only advancement for me at BOCES would be to become the Director of

Special Education. However, there was already an Assistant Director who was poised to take that position; in fact, he did take it when the original Director retired. My mind was flooded with thoughts again that I had to find another position that would provide me with an opportunity to grow and once again prove my worth.

Executive Director: Pathways Inc.: There was a private nonprofit agency in our community called Pathways, Inc. Several of the students with severe mental retardation who were in the BOCES school, where I served as principal, eventually progressed to the Day Treatment program operated by Pathways. The BOCES psychologist working with the emotionally disturbed students was on the board at the agency and informed me that the position of Executive Director was vacant and they were in an active search for a replacement. This was immediately of interest to me. I had worked for the public schools, the State Office of Mental Health and BOCES. Working for a private community agency would add a new dimension for me. I believed that I had enough of a variety of experiences at that point to be able to do a good job as an Executive Director.

In March of 1985 I interviewed for the Executive Director position. The interview team consisted of four Pathways Board members and the local county Director of Mental Health. I knew him well from my years at the Psychiatric Center. I was very comfortable with the interview. The questions seemed to be in areas where I had experience and the interview team appeared pleased with my answers.

After the interview I returned to my BOCES office and worked there until approximately seven o'clock that night. Before I left I received a phone call from the president of the Pathways Board of Directors. He was calling to offer me the position and to ask me to meet with him and another board member for breakfast at the Hilton in Corning the next morning. He said, "I would like you to think about, and come prepared to discuss, what it would take to get you to accept this position." I was blown away by that approach. None of my previous positions would ever allow for that type of discussion to occur. Both for the state and the school districts there could be some negotiations about salary range, but the other benefits were pretty much set for everyone.

That night Peggy and I prayed about the decision and had some serious discussions about the pros and cons of accepting the position. I also called a friend who was experienced in the business world and asked his advice about what I should be trying to achieve in the breakfast meeting. We agreed that there were two serious issues. One, Pathways had only a minimal type of retirement plan. It was tremendously inferior to the New York State Teachers' Retirement Plan that I was a member of at the time. Secondly, the health insurance plan at Pathways was very substandard in comparison to the one I had at BOCES.

At the breakfast meeting, we were able to resolve the issues around my retirement, but they told me that if I accepted the position one of my first duties would be to find a better health insurance plan for myself and the rest of the employees. As for the salary, the top of their range was close to my current salary and I was willing to accept it. Before we concluded the meeting I accepted the position.

My first day on the job as Executive Director was April 15, 1985. At that time Pathways operated two day treatment programs and one community residence, all for adults with developmental disabilities. Additionally, a family support services program for families with developmentally disabled children was in the formative stage. There was great freedom for me in this new position. There was no formal structure such as a school district or New York State Office as there was at the State operated facility at the psychiatric center. The services at Pathways were regulated by the New York State Office of Mental Retardation and Developmental Disabilities [OMRDD], but there were no State employees present every day.

The fact that Pathways was a private agency allowed for much freedom to develop any service covered within its bylaws. During my first month on the job, the Pathways Board of Directors charged me with the responsibility for assessing the current status of the agency and development of a draft for a five-year plan. In the process of carrying out that task, I met with several people from the local community and from the OMRDD. I also met with the directors of the various Association for Retarded Citizens [ARC's] and United Cerebral Palsy Association, since they served a similar clientele as Pathways. I tried to determine what separated us from the other agencies serving individuals with developmental disabilities.

I discovered that there were two important distinguishing factors that would prove to be guiding principles for years to come. First, Pathways was noted for providing services for the moderate to severely impaired individuals. The ARC's usually served mild to moderately disabled individuals at that time. The second and possibly most important, distinguishing difference was the fact that Pathways' bylaws allowed the agency to consider the development of services that were not solely for people with developmental disabilities. That meant that the agency could develop a broader base of services and operate with a variety of funding sources as opposed to relying solely on OMRDD.

The proposed five-year plan I presented to the board in 1985 included expansion into the mental health field as well as elder care services. After the Board approved the plan, I met with state and local professionals from the mental health field who I had been associated with in my other positions. I began to lay the groundwork for potential new developments in mental health in case the state or counties were looking for a community agency to expand their services. In due time that sort of networking paid off because Pathways was eventually invited to submit a proposal to operate a Professional Foster Care program for emotionally disturbed children. We were in competition with agencies that were solely mental health in nature; however, we were selected much to the amazement of the other providers.

I also began to serve on a local board comprised of members from various other human service agencies in the county. My intent was to assist in any way I could in the improvement of service delivery for the county and, also, to become aware of service needs in the area in order for Pathways to consider program expansion. I know that some of my associates considered my involvement on this and other boards to be a waste of time and a distraction from what they thought I should be doing. Perhaps I could have been doing other things that would have helped the agency, but these activities did lead to development of several new services for Pathways over the next seventeen and a half years. However, I believed this was a major part of my responsibilities. These relationships ultimately led to Pathways being invited to submit applications to operate a number of new programs. For years the agency had a track record of always being selected each time we submitted a proposal. The agency reputation was superb.

My Greatest Satisfaction from My Employment

All through my professional career I strived to be the best I could possibly be, no matter what my task. It was always my goal to do things in a manner that was different, innovative or creative so that the programs stood out from the rest. At Elmira Psychiatric Center I was blessed to be a part of the team that developed an innovative community-based psycho-educational program for children and youth which was awarded the recognition as the best program in the state at the time. At BOCES, I had the opportunity to be the principal of a special school for emotionally disturbed children and youth and also for developmentally disabled students. Even though it was a special school, we were able to bring in outside groups to prevent it from being so isolated.

At Pathways it was my privilege to lead the agency through major growth from three programs to forty- three programs over a seventeen and a half year period. The agency grew from approximately sixty to approximately four hundred fifty staff. It progressed into three divisions including Developmental Disability Services, Mental Health Services and Child and Family Services. The operating budget grew from less than one million in 1985 to over fifteen million dollars per year in 2002. It was widely recognized for quality services and was selected by Corning Incorporated [formerly Corning Glass Works] to operate some of its child care services. Pathways was distinguished in that it was a multi-service agency attempting to meet the diverse needs of the people in our surrounding communities.

The Interlude

The next phase of my life I refer to as The Interlude. The dictionary defines interlude as a short piece between two longer pieces, as in a musical arrangement. It is also described as an intervening episode. Of course, as my life was progressing, I didn't know those years were intervening between anything. For the most part we see life moving forward at a steady pace. But, as I am able to look back, I can easily see now that portions of the years 1999, 2000 and 2001 were, in actuality, a break from the life I had become accustomed to and the life that would follow starting at the end of 2001.

There were two powerful forces working in my life that made this time period a living nightmare. One force was a set of physical symptoms that nearly permanently sidelined me, and the second was intense emotional distress leading to severe depression. The physical symptoms began first, followed by the emotional distress. Eventually, the two seemed to be intertwined, and I am sure that the physical problems were magnified by the emotional distress.

Complicated Physical Problems

During 1999, I began to have a series of physical problems that were very difficult to deal with on a daily basis. The first sign of a problem came as I was leaving for work one morning. I turned around near the front door to say goodbye to Peggy and nearly fell forward onto the floor. I was dizzy and became a little nauseous. If that had been the only incident like that I probably wouldn't have even remembered it. However, there started to be numerous incidents of dizziness, vertigo and coordination problems. Soon I began walking into door casings at home and at work. At first it seemed a little comical and people laughed along with me. Eventually, however, when I began falling for no apparent reason, I knew there was something wrong that needed to be checked out.

In early 2000, I made an appointment with my primary physician to report the physical symptoms I was having. He conducted a few simple neurological tests in his office and ordered an MRI of my brain. As I was driving home from work a few days after the MRI, I received a phone call from the doctor's nurse. She told me that the result had come in regarding my brain scan and the doctor wanted me to come in the next morning to discuss it. I said, "Am I to assume that there is a problem?" She replied that she was not at liberty to discuss the findings with me, but there was something that the doctor wanted to check out a little further. I had an extremely important meeting the next morning and requested that we meet in the afternoon instead. She confirmed that I could come in around 3:00 PM and the doctor would try to fit me into his schedule. Needless to say, the time between that phone call and the appointment were anxious hours.

When I got home and explained the phone message to Peggy we immediately sat down and prayed about the situation. I think we both were sincere about trusting the Lord with the problem. We were always quick to bring our problems to the Lord and not get panicky about things, but it was hard to not worry somewhat about what the doctor was going to tell me the next day.

The appointment could not come fast enough for us. Although we didn't verbalize it out loud, I know we were both concerned that perhaps there was some type of tumor causing the symptoms. When the time finally arrived for my appointment there was a lot of drama. I was sitting alone in the examining room as my doctor and his nurse came in together, closed the door and sat down. The doctor asked me how I was feeling and inquired if I had had any more of the symptoms I reported earlier. I explained that I had. He informed me that the MRI had detected a lesion near the Pons area of my brain and that there were various other slightly darkened spots scattered throughout the brain. I, of course, inquired if he thought it was a brain tumor, to which he replied that it was inconclusive at that time. He reported that it didn't appear to be a tumor, but further testing was going to have to be done.

At that point my doctor asked if I was familiar with multiple sclerosis or MS. I explained that as part of my college training I had studied about MS, but that I didn't have any vast understanding about it. He asked whether I knew if anyone else in my family had MS. I responded that I did not and asked if he thought that I had it. He replied that it was too soon to tell, but that my symptoms and the MRI were indicative of MS. He suggested that I could get some books about MS from the library or buy some at the local bookstore to see if I thought my symptoms were anything like what was described about the disorder. He told me that he was going to refer me to a neurologist who would conduct further testing. He had his staff make the appointment but, unfortunately, it was going to be three weeks before the neurologist could see me.

I did go straight to the bookstore and purchased two books about MS. The next several days Peggy and I studied them thoroughly. It seemed as though I had most of the symptoms that were noted for the disorder. We were particularly interested in what forms of treatment were available and how disabling it might become. The first thing we noticed was that it was very complicated to diagnose and that there were various forms, each affecting a person differently.

Appointment with First Neurologist: I finally had my appointment with the neurologist who ordered several more tests, some of them quite painful. The most painful one was the spinal tap. The neurologist inserted her needle three or four times and expressed exasperation that she wasn't able to get much spinal fluid. Finally, she stepped into the hallway and summoned a nurse and asked for the "longest needle they had." By this time I was shaking like a leaf and you could hear the rails on the gurney rattle. Finally, with the long needle she seemed to be satisfied, but the pain was unbearable for me. Her last comment to me was, "Why you shake so much?" With that she left and did not return. After about fifteen minutes of lying there alone, I sat up and waited until my head stopped spinning. I stepped to the open doorway and looked for someone to ask if I was finished. Seeing no one I got dressed and sat down until I saw a nurse in the hall. I asked her if I was free to go. After I explained that I had just had a spinal tap she said, " Well, I guess you can go then." What a weird experience!

The neurologist had ordered several more neurological evaluations as well. After three weeks, I went back for a follow-up appointment to get the results of all the testing, including the spinal tap. Peggy and I waited in the examining room for over a half hour for the neurologist to come in. We thought this would be the day we would know if I had MS or not. When she entered she had my chart in her hands and said, "So, what brings you here today?" More than a little shocked I replied, "We came to get the results of all the testing you ordered about a month ago. You were trying to determine whether or not I have MS." She quickly leafed through the chart and got up and left the room without saying a word.

Peggy and I sat in the room for approximately thirty more minutes waiting. The door was open and we saw my doctor walk by a few times. It was clear that she was seeing other patients. It seems that she had not seen the results of my testing and was waiting for them to be sent from another department so that she could review them and then come back to speak to us. However, neither she nor anyone else came to tell us what we were waiting for. Finally, she came back into the room and simply said that all my testing results were in the normal range and that she would forward that information back to my primary physician. She wished us a nice day and quickly left the room.

I was overwhelmed at that point. I now had a full-fledged migraine and was experiencing some of the dizziness that had been part of my ongoing problems. I could barely walk unassisted at this point in the progression of my symptoms. Peggy held on to my arm as we left the clinic and I promised I would never return there again. I had incredible frustration because all of my symptoms were getting progressively worse and yet the neurological testing showed that all was within the normal range. I began to have coordination difficulties and visual disturbances as well. If I sat in my car in a line of traffic it appeared to me that the vehicles in front of me were moving up and down. This phenomenon often made me nauseous and I had to look away. I was often bothered by a sensation of seeing movement in my peripheral vision. When I turned to see what was moving, there was nothing moving.

By the time I returned for an appointment with my primary physician, approximately a month after the appointment with the neurologist, I was experiencing frequent falls. I felt as though my legs weighed a ton and I found it an effort to even walk in the grass because it felt like it was tripping me up. Most of my falling was outside fortunately. My physician suggested that I purchase a cane to try to maintain balance and keep from falling. I had also developed a tremor, mostly in my right hand. I had difficulty sleeping because I would lie awake with the sensation that there were bugs crawling inside my legs.

Referral to Boston: In 2001, since my symptoms were continuing and getting more severe, my physician decided to refer me to the Neurology Department at Brigham and Women's Hospital in Boston. He was familiar with some of the doctors there and knew they specialized in diagnosing MS and other low incidence syndromes. Peggy and I were pleased that we were going to have a very good chance of finding out what was causing all my physical problems.

The results of all of my testing, including my MRI, were sent on ahead to Boston. Two doctors spent a long time examining me and going over my records. At the conclusion of the appointment they determined that I did not have MS. They said that it appeared that I had one of any number of low incidence syndromes that were characterized by symptoms similar to mine. They said that I could stay and be tested over a period of several days and perhaps go home with a name for what I had, but the fact was that the treatment would be the same. If I could be comfortable knowing that I did not have MS and not having a name for my disorder, they would recommend a combination of medications to try to control the symptoms.

Secondly, the primary physician there in Boston strongly suggested that I stop drinking caffeinated coffee since caffeine exaggerates the symptoms even more. At that time I was drinking at least eight cups per day. I unwisely stopped "cold turkey" and went through two weeks of miserable withdrawal. I never realized how addicted I was to caffeine. I had always thought I could easily stop any time I wanted. I began to wonder if that was the cause of all the symptoms, but then I remembered the lesion on the brain and realized that there must be something more.

The absence of the caffeine in my body did seem to reduce the severity of my problems for quite a while. However, eventually all the symptoms were still there. Probably the most disturbing ones were the falling and the balance and coordination problems. My physician referred me for physical therapy to deal with these issues. I was taken through numerous types of activities to try to improve balance and muscle coordination. Additionally, some of the physical therapy was geared at strengthening my leg muscles. The therapist told me that my leg muscles were very stiff, almost like iron. I completed many exercises to try to loosen them up. I was also given activities to do at home.

Referral to Strong Memorial in Rochester, New York: After several months of the new medications suggested by the doctor in Boston I was still having a very significant number of the original symptoms. At that point, in late 2002, my primary physician referred me to an epidemiologist at the Strong Memorial Hospital in Rochester, New York. I had two appointments there. The first was for an actual physical examination and the second was to receive a report of his findings. Since Strong Memorial is a training hospital, the epidemiology department often brings unusual cases before a team of doctors and interns for review. My records from all of the testing and treatment over the past year or two were available for them to review.

When Peggy and I went for the second visit the doctor told us that he felt relatively certain that they had discovered the cause of all of my symptoms. He indicated that his team had reviewed all of the X-rays, MRI films and other test results as well as reports from other physicians who had examined me. He reported that they believed that the lesion and other dark spots on the brain were the result of my almost lifelong complex migraine headaches. I had had severe migraines since my teen years and intermittently all through my adult life too. During these migraines I often had numbness in my face, tongue, hand and arm, along with extreme visual anomalies resulting in nausea and vomiting and finally, of course, a severe headache.

The doctor explained that during these periods of severe and complex migraines the blood supply to the brain would be drastically restricted. Eventually, the lack of blood resulted in the death of the cells at the very ends of the tiny vessels in the brain. Whatever physical functions those cells were supposed to be controlling would now be affected. The dark areas on the MRI were those areas of dead cells. He explained that while his diagnosis sounded very serious, it was not as threatening as it sounded. He further explained that the brain is an amazing organ in that it has the ability to heal itself or to at least find new pathways to perform the functions once performed by cells that have now died.

His final determination was that, although he could not go in surgically and repair the brain, he could recommend medications to help control or stop the migraines so no further damage would be done. He sent his report to my primary physician and the medication changes were implemented. Some of the medications originally recommended by the Boston doctor were also continued. The Rochester doctor warned that we should not expect overnight changes, but that there should be a gradual decrease in the symptoms as the migraines were reduced in intensity and frequency.

By the end of 2002 I was definitely experiencing a reduction in the intensity of the migraines. However, I was still having most of the physical symptoms that I had experienced for the previous two years. The tremor, lack of balance, and falling were still an ongoing struggle for me.

The Emotional Distress

In addition to the physical issues I was dealing with during 1999-2001, I was also trying to cope with significantly increased depression. The physical problems were, in and of themselves, enough to cause depression. Additionally, there were various personnel issues at work that frustrated me. I had worked for sixteen years in a job that I loved, and yet I was struggling to see how I would be able to continue my lifelong practice of succeeding and achieving in order to prove my worth. I felt as though I was failing to meet my own standards as well as the standards of some of my co-workers. I began to be paranoid and distrustful of some of the people with whom I should have been able to work closely.

Stressful Events

I am not trying to make excuses for what ultimately happened in my life, but I do think that there were certain events that figured into the state of mind that I was in that contributed to my downfall. I describe them here simply as a caution to the reader to beware that when major emotional pressures are present, we are much more vulnerable to Satan's attacks.

Public Meetings: In the summer of 1999 Pathways conducted public meetings regarding the establishment of two new residences for the individuals we served. In each case the location of the facilities was unpopular with the neighbors surrounding the properties. As the Executive Director, it was my responsibility to stand in front of the crowd and make a presentation and answer questions afterward. In both of these situations the crowd response was overwhelmingly negative. I was heckled, called a liar and generally shown tremendous disrespect by many of those in attendance. I was interviewed on television, radio and by the local newspapers. In each case I found it difficult to physically stand for the time period of the meeting. We did ultimately make it through the approval process, but not without substantial strain on me. I hasten to add that it was worth the stress I had to endure to be able to secure the permission we needed to provide the much needed residences for the locations in question.

Death of our niece: In September of 1999 our family received a devastating shock when our twenty-three year old niece, who lived next door on the family farm, was tragically killed in an automobile accident on her way home from work. She was married to Peggy's nephew, who was one of the brothers who operated the farm that had been in Peggy's family for over 100 years. We were very close as a family and saw each other on a regular basis each week. Having recently fulfilled her dream to become a nurse, she was on her way home after working all night at a local hospital. One never expects to lose someone that young. The impact on all of the family was major.

The Past Becomes the Present: Sometime late in 2000, an event occurred that brought the horrors of my childhood sexual abuse to the forefront and became a new set of devastating circumstances for me to cope with. The next series of events I want to describe are still part of this Interlude I am talking about; however, these events necessarily bleed into the rest of my life.

I preface this section with the acknowledgement that Peggy and I were some of last holdouts when it came to getting the Internet into our house. We had heard and read some stories about the negative side of the Internet, particularly the ease at which pornography can be found freely. However, we finally gave in to the "need" to have it because so much of our society was now tied to the Internet. When we first got connected to the Internet it was mostly to use email, check the weather or to search some topic we wanted to learn about. Later, for me it became a major source of news information that I usually couldn't find on the television.

I began using the Internet from time to time as I was preparing Sunday school lessons for the adult class I taught at our church. It was during one of my Internet searches for my lesson that I came upon a website that changed the course of my life and that of my family and loved ones as well.

One evening, as I was doing an Internet search on the topic of demonology, my computer screen became filled with a series of pop-ups. I had been on various other sites and had gained some valuable information on the topic. However, when I clicked on an additional one, my searching came to an end. My computer screen started filling up with pop-up images, one on top of another. Each time I clicked on the "red x" in the upper right corner of the images it only brought more images to the screen. The images were grotesque pictures of animal sacrifice, humans hanging upside down with their insides bursting out and then one final image that came to rest in the front and center of my screen. It was an image containing child pornography. It contained a picture of three teenage boys who seemed to be in a tent or at least had some type of fabric draped behind them. Two of the boys were performing sexual acts on the third boy who was in the middle. It was strikingly similar to what had happened to me as a twelve year old on my first camp out. It had the name of a website printed across the bottom which was easy for me to remember because it contained the word "buddies." That was the name my first childhood abuser called me when I was four and five years of age.

I was shocked and sickened by all of the images, but especially this last one. I called for Peggy to come down to my office to see what had happened. Again I tried to get rid of the images, but more kept coming. Ultimately, I had to manually turn off the computer in order to stop this process. When I tried to reboot the computer it would not complete the process. A window opened indicating that one of the required files necessary to reboot had been deleted. It was necessary to take the computer to a technician to restore the proper file. He indicated that most likely the website that had brought the images to my screen had also corrupted the files on the computer.

The Aftermath: The frustration of having my computer file corrupted was the least of the impact this event had on me. Already depressed and emotionally weakened in the midst of some severe physical problems, I was now overwhelmed by the rush of painful memories that image of the three boys had on me. I was also puzzled because the boy who one would think was the victim did not seem in any way distressed by what was happening to him. It started me thinking that perhaps my first abuser was actually correct and this is "what boys do." If that was true, then perhaps I wasn't such a bad person after all. My thoughts would waiver between thinking, "No, this is bad, no matter how you look at it," to "Well, if everyone does stuff like that, I am not the worthless piece of 'sh__' my teenage abusers said that I am." It was very confusing to me and the thoughts about it were almost continuously on my mind over the next several days.

About two weeks after the images popped up on my screen, I was working late at night in my office at home and Peggy had already gone to bed. My mind was flooded with the image that I had seen. The name of the website was ever present in my head because of the word "buddies" included in it. Then I made the mistake that would forever change my life. I typed in the name of the website and then sat there with my finger over the enter key. I actually prayed, "Father, forgive me, but I have to know more about this website." I knew that to visit that site would be morally wrong, but I was weak and overwhelmed by my emotions.

I hit the enter key and immediately saw the same image that had popped up a couple weeks before. Then I saw the word "enter" and again I paused and asked for God's forgiveness before hitting that key. Now I realize how ridiculous that was. God does not work that way. We cannot know that we are going to intentionally sin and ask God to forgive us in advance. That is an indication of how stressed out and how clouded my thinking had become.

What Was This Website? I discovered that the website was a bulletin board. Anyone could post anything they wanted on the site. Messages were simply listed and numbered and one would not know what he was going to see until he clicked on a numbered entry. I began clicking and found that there were more images similar to the one I had seen, but there were also messages that attracted my attention. There were messages from men who said they had been abused as children and they were now condemning this site for posting the pictures. They described how their childhood abuse had affected them throughout their whole lives. Other messages were from people condemning those who had said they had been abused, calling them hypocrites since they were visiting the site too. I tended to believe those who said they were abused since I could relate to the feelings they were describing.

I never posted any comments to the site and, furthermore, never knew how one would do that even if I was so inclined, which I was not. I was simply a bystander on the sidelines. I was intrigued by the comments from the men who said they had been abused. I had never spoken to, nor ever heard about, any man who would admit he had been abused and was finally talking about it. It became a form of relief for me to read those comments. Every time I visited the site I also saw more of the images as well. I couldn't avoid it since it was never clear when you clicked on a number in the list if it was going to be a picture or a written message. I never saw an image where the participants looked distressed. This continued to confuse me.

Eventually, over the next year I would visit this website a couple of times per month and others too, that were recommended on this first one. They all seemed to work the same way. The guilt from being drawn to visit them became very strong. I realize now that Satan had used something that he knew would be like "bait" for me to lure me into a sinful habit of visiting this and other similar websites. I reached a point where I was totally miserable as a result of this struggle. Each time I visited a website I would leave after a very few minutes and cry and plead with God for forgiveness. And then I would ask for His forgiveness for what I saw as a horrible habit of sinning and repenting over and over again. What I thought was something that was going to help me understand myself better became a snare from which I could not break free. I had given ground to Satan and I could not take it back on my own.

God Intervenes: On November 17, 2001, after approximately a year of this sin/repent cycle, I became so overwhelmed with despair and guilt that I crawled into the kneehole of my desk at home and, with my face on the floor, pleaded with God to rescue me from the trap I knew I was in. I thought I knew how it could happen and had a plan in my mind. I thought I would tell Peggy all about my childhood abuse, its impact on my life, my sinful habit with the Internet and then have the Internet disconnected and seek counseling from a Christian counselor.

As usually happens, God had a better plan. Two days later November 19, 2001, before I was able to institute my plan,

God intervened. Peggy and I were finishing our morning devotions together before I would rush off for a dental appointment and she would be greeting a number of ladies coming for a Bible study. Much to our shock and dismay, we saw three unmarked cars pull into our driveway and two State Police cars pull across the entrance. State Police got out and started running to the sides and back of our house and one was coming toward the front door with a large maul in his hands. Two men wearing FBI jackets emerged from the unmarked cars that had driven down the driveway. I immediately went to the door to see what was going on. I knew that there had been some break-ins in our area and I thought this might have something to do with that. I asked the men wearing FBI jackets, "What is going on here?" One of them answered, "You don't have any idea why we are here?" I said, "Does this have something to do with the robberies that have been going on around here?" One of them replied, "No, but do you know of anyone in this house who might be accessing websites containing child pornography?" I admitted that I had visited sites like that, but they were free websites and I hadn't printed or made files of any of the material on those sites. He indicated that they had a search warrant and that they were there to search our home for child pornography. I told them that they were welcome to do that because I knew they would find nothing.

Once inside the house the FBI agents kept Peggy in the living room and escorted me to the family room. They had a State Policeman stay with Peggy while two others searched all the rooms in the house plus the garage, basement and a shed behind the house. They had entered the house with several cardboard boxes, apparently assuming there would be plenty to take out. Peggy was totally confused about what was going on. She asked the policeman who was with her and he eventually told her that he thought it had something to do with the computer. At one point I asked to speak to Peggy and suggested she call the ladies who were supposed to be coming for Bible study to head them off for that day. I also asked her to phone the dentist to let him know I would not be in that morning.

Eventually, after nearly an hour of questioning me, the FBI agent asked to see my computer. During the questioning period I naively responded very truthfully to all of the questions asked. The agent told me that all would go better for me if I willingly cooperated. I had always operated under the assumption that honesty is the best policy. I did not believe that I was in any serious trouble since I had only visited the website and viewed the postings there. The site was free and I had never downloaded the images into files, forwarded them or printed them out. Furthermore, I had deleted the history and temporary Internet files upon shutting down the computer every time because I did not want anyone to be able to say I was keeping the images. So, I believed I had not done anything illegal.

The FBI agent went into my computer and quickly began checking out various files. He did not find the images that he was looking for. While he was searching I sat at Peggy's desk across from mine and stared out the window. At one point I said, "Thank God it's over." He replied by saying, "Oh, I'm afraid it's far from over for you sir." He had no idea about what my statement meant to me. I knew that there might be some rough days ahead, but I assumed that finally my lifetime secret was going to come out in the open, at least to a select group, and that I would be released from the Internet trap and would be free at last.

The agent removed the hard drive from my computer and placed it in his pocket. Meanwhile the second agent showed me some photographs of child pornography and asked if I had ever seen any of them online. I pointed out a couple of them that I recalled seeing. I made their jobs very easy. They also asked me to write a statement confessing what I had done as far as visiting the website was concerned. Again, I thought I had done nothing illegal and that my truthful responses would be best as they would see I had nothing to hide. Before leaving they also took my laptop computer and asked me to show them to my office at Pathways. On the way out I asked if I could speak to Peggy alone. While they waited outside I knelt down in front of my confused and horrified beloved Peggy. She asked what was going on. In the briefest of ways, I tried to explain and then told her I would come right back home after showing these agents to my office. She asked, "Are you going to lose your job?" I replied, "No, I doubt there will be any problem when they find out more." I hugged and kissed her and promised to be right back.

On the way to the office I prayed constantly that the Lord would rescue me from this horrible situation and that He would spare me public humiliation and loss of my job. Once at the office the agents removed the hard drive from my computer and left. I informed my Administrative Assistant that I was leaving and would not be back that day. I returned home to console Peggy. I had a lot of explaining to do.

I called this section of my story the Interlude because it was a vast departure from all that had gone on before it, but was mild compared with what would now follow. Those events will be told in Part Two.

Part Two

CONSEQUENCES AND VICTORY

Chapter 8

THE FIRST SIX WEEKS OF TURMOIL

An Attorney and a Christian Counselor

Back Home: After I came back from my office, I again knelt down on the floor in front of Peggy and began to tell her my whole story, from childhood abuse, its impact on me through the years and the snare I believed I had become trapped in with the Internet over the past year. I was fearful that she would be angry and full of disgust for me and my actions. I wouldn't have blamed her if she did feel that way. On the contrary, while she did not approve of what I had done, she immediately began to support me. She kept asking, "Why didn't you ever tell me you were in such turmoil over this?" She said, "I would have tried to help you in some way."

I explained to Peggy that I had always believed that I had done a terrible thing as a child and that if anyone ever found out I would be ostracized. I was fearful that even she would find me to be repulsive. I explained that I always had to be achieving and successful in order to prove my worth. I shared that I always tried to make people pleased with me out of fear of being rejected. That habit often left me caught in the middle during conflicts between other people, but also brought me the reputation of being a peacemaker.

Peggy shared her concern once again that I might lose my job. I tried to assure her that I didn't believe that would happen because I didn't think I had done anything illegal. Furthermore, the FBI had not found any child pornography anywhere in the house. Nevertheless, we agreed that I needed to contact an attorney immediately to discuss the whole situation, particularly since the FBI agent told me I would be receiving a letter from the Federal Prosecutor's office in a few days.

It would have been our normal response at this point to call our pastor to let him know what was going on and ask for his prayer support. However, he and his wife had just left that morning for a week of vacation. We certainly did not want to burden them with this and, besides, there was always the possibility that nothing serious would come of it since the police search did not result in them finding anything.

Contacting An Attorney: We agreed on the attorney I would call in order to discuss the situation. He was one I had worked with over the several years I had worked in Chemung County, New York. I had great respect for him as a person and as a professional. We were not disappointed. I phoned him around noon and he was able to see us at 2:00 PM that same day.

In our meeting with the attorney I once again explained the whole story from my childhood to the present situation. As I expected, he was non-judgmental and supportive. He initially agreed that he did not believe that there was anything illegal about what I had done. He cautioned us, however, that there still might be some negative publicity and we should be prepared for that. He asked that we give him time to research the law regarding this type of thing, and we agreed that we would meet again in a few days.

I explained to the attorney that my nephew, who lived next door, had come down to our house immediately when the police pulled in. I had told him that everything was ok and that he could go back home. Also, Peggy, while sitting in our living room as the FBI questioned me in another room, saw several cars, belonging to people we knew, slow down and stare at our house. I questioned him about what we should say if asked about what was going on. He suggested that we not divulge any information at this point since the whole thing might end up being dismissed. He suggested we could simply say, "it is not anything we are at liberty to discuss right now."

Contacting A Christian Counselor: That same afternoon, I contacted a Christian counselor who was also a long-time friend. He was able to meet with us the next morning. Once again, I went through my whole story, this time very tearfully because I was also talking about it not just from a legal standpoint, but from a sin standpoint. I was extremely repentant and prayed right then, admitting my sinful behavior on the Internet and asking for God's forgiveness and cleansing from such unrighteousness. I had already prayed that type of prayer at home, in fact many times, only to repeat the same sinful behavior again soon thereafter. The difference now was that it was in the presence of Peggy and a man I greatly respected. There was a new type of accountability available now. The counselor shared some very important and valuable scriptures from 1 Peter chapter 5 with us. We discussed them and then prayed together. We agreed that we would meet again the following week.

Before we left the meeting with the counselor he suggested that we not tell anyone else about what was going on at this point. We had no idea what was going to happen and his recommendation was that we just "sit tight for now."

Disconnecting the Internet

One of the next important decisions we made was to have the Internet disconnected from our computer. I made the request to our provider the next day after the FBI visit. That was a move that I had planned as part of my solution to my problem before God implemented His plan. I cannot express the relief that I felt knowing that it was no longer available to me. I felt badly for Peggy because she was just becoming comfortable using it for various purposes. It was just one of many ways that she would end up suffering the consequences of my sin.

Journaling

Peggy and my counselor strongly suggested that I start keeping a journal on a regular basis. I had never done anything like that before, but decided that it might be helpful for me to get my thoughts and emotions identified on paper. I am so happy that I followed their suggestion. At various times through this part of my account I will insert my journal entry for the day because it may be the best way to demonstrate the impact the whole event was having on me at the time.

The following entry represents my reaction to the scripture verses that our counselor shared at our first appointment.

Journal Entry
November 20, 2001

One Day after the FBI Came to our House

"Likewise, ye younger, submit yourselves unto the elder. Yea, all of you be subject one to another, and be clothed with humility: for God resisteth the proud, and giveth grace to the humble. Humble yourselves therefore under the mighty hand of God, that He may exalt you in due time:" 1 Peter 5:5-6

I think that being humble sometimes requires being humiliated first. In my present situation I have been humbled by having to admit my sin, first to Peggy, and then to two other people I have always respected. It was very hard to do, but absolutely necessary to start my healing process. I long for God's grace in this situation.

There is no power stronger than "God's mighty hand." To humble myself under His mighty hand is an awesome thought. I believe His hand is more powerful than my problems and more powerful than anything else anywhere.

"Casting all your care upon Him; for He careth for you." 1 Peter 5:7

Casting all of my cares on Him means I have to let go. I have to trust that He is able to carry them to the end, and that it will be for my good. I have to have faith in Him explicitly. I pray that I can let go of the worry and trust Him with everything. I pray that my dear Peggy will be able to do the same. I think she will, because I have never met anyone who trusts God more than she does. I cast all my cares on Him now.

I feel an intense need to protect Peggy. She did nothing wrong and yet will suffer innocently for my wrong doing. I will accept whatever God wills for my life, but I pray for her protection from further hurt, if that is possible. She is already hurt from the events so far.

"Be sober, be vigilant; because your adversary the devil, as a roaring lion, walketh about, seeking whom he may devour:" 1 Peter 5:8

Sober or self-controlled and alert: Self control, or lack of it, has been a real problem for me. If I would have been more vigilant and watchful of Satan's attempts to trip me up, I would not be in the situation I find myself in right now. I have not been alert to Satan's tactics, or else I have ignored them. The sad thing is, I can easily see his tactics at work luring others into sin, but have been blind to his devious methods as they have influenced me and led me to make bad choices.

Roaring lion, seeking to devour: I have allowed Satan to attack me and he has knocked me down, but I will not allow him to devour me. I cannot prevent this on my own; I will require and accept the mighty hand of God over me. His mighty hand will easily prevent Satan from devouring me. I trust that whatever God allows to happen will be for my good and His glory.

"Whom resist steadfast in the faith, knowing that the same afflictions are accomplished in your brethren that are in the world." 1 Peter 5:9

Resist Satan and stand firm in faith: All through God's word it is clear that when we place our trust in Him He will deliver us from our tribulation. I am resisting the devil; the major source of my trouble, the Internet, has literally been removed from my grasp, and I have confessed openly to the right people, who will help to hold me accountable. I am seeking wise counsel from a Godly man who uses the Word of God as the basis for all his counseling.

The passage says that brothers throughout the world are undergoing the same type of suffering. I understand 1 Corinthians 10:13 and how it applies here. God provided the way for me to escape the temptation and I failed to follow that way. I'm in a deep trial of my own making. Yet, I know that 1 Corinthians 10:13 still applies. He will not give Peggy and me more than we can handle through Him. I claim that promise now and rest on it. I accept the possibility that His way out of my troubles may mean a dramatic change in our lives in some way.

"But the God of all grace, who hath called us unto His eternal glory by Christ Jesus, after that ye have suffered for a while, make you perfect, stablish, strengthen, settle you." 1 Peter 5:10

The God of all grace: I praise Him for His matchless grace and love for me. I should be dead now, but for His grace and mercy. I believe it is because of this same grace that He will see me through this trial. By His grace, I will not fail this test.

He called me to His eternal glory. I believe that He has not changed His plan for me or my eternal destination. I have currently thwarted His plan for me. However, the utmost desire of my life is to return to walking in His perfect will. I have already repented and been forgiven. I have asked Him to restore and cleanse me from all my unrighteousness. In faith, I believe that has already happened.

After I have suffered a little while: Whew! I hate that thought. This is the hardest part for me, yet I willingly accept the suffering. I know that He is just and I have already claimed 1 Corinthians 10:13. I also know that suffering is like the "refiner's fire." It only works to make me stronger and mature. If suffering is necessary to purify my heart and mature my walk in Him, then I say, "Bring it on!"

After the suffering He will restore me, make me strong, firm and steadfast. This promise makes all the suffering worthwhile. He will restore me. He says He will and that is final. I must keep myself pure and feed on His Word so that He can work in and through me. I want to be a very positive witness for Christ throughout all that may be ahead.

"To Him be glory and dominion forever and ever. Amen." 1 Peter 5:11

His power is what makes my faith strong. His power is matchless [the same as His grace and mercy]. Amen, so be it.

The greatest area of weakness for me now is my inability to prevent Satan from defeating me with fear of the future consequences of my actions. However, I will not allow fear to pull me down because I also claim *Romans 8:28 "And we know that all things work together for good to them that love God, to them who are called according to His purpose."*

He will bring me into a better place in the end. It may be restoration or it may be movement into a place and work totally different, but it will be for my good and His glory. I believe this with all my heart and this truth will keep fear from defeating me.

Letter from the U.S. Attorney's Office:

On November 23, 2001, I received the official letter from the United States District Court for the Middle District of

Pennsylvania. It was something that really shook my world. If I thought having the FBI show up and search my house was terrifying, this letter was even more of a blow. We no longer wondered if my actions would be considered illegal. The front page of the letter boldly stated:

The United States of America   Criminal No. 000000000

v.

Bruce D. Hughes

The letter noted dates of the alleged criminal act and pointed out that the penalty for such an act could be up to five years of incarceration and a $250,000 fine. Needless to say, Peggy and I were devastated. At this point we had not told anyone about this situation other than our counselor and attorney. There was no one else we could turn to at the moment of receipt of the letter other than each other and, of course, the Lord.

I had always been a patriotic citizen who was proud of my country. I had not missed voting in primary and general elections for as long as I could remember. To receive a letter stating The United States of America versus Bruce D. Hughes was almost more than I could handle. I could not believe that it could possibly be true. The thought that I had done something that made me appear to be on the opposite side of my country was beyond belief.

Journal Entry
November 23, 2001

The Lord reminded me of the account of Manasseh in 2 Kings 21 and 2 Chronicles 33. Manasseh reversed all the good things that his father, Hezekiah, had done in terms of eliminating filthy idols from Israel. He even brought a sexual idol into the temple. He had God's prophets slaughtered until Jerusalem was overflowing with blood.

Ultimately, God allowed Manasseh to be taken captive by the king of Assyria. He had a ring placed in Manasseh's nose and led him through the streets in great humiliation. *2 Chronicles 33:12-13 "And when he was in affliction, he besought the Lord his God, and humbled himself greatly before the God of his fathers, and prayed unto Him: and He was entreated of him, and heard his supplication, and brought him again to Jerusalem into his kingdom. Then Manasseh knew that the Lord He was God."*

I see here that recovery begins with shame. I understand that to be ashamed is an important first step to repentance. Manasseh took full responsibility for all the terrible wrong he had done and then humbled himself greatly. The Lord restored Manasseh and Manasseh tore down the idols and turned back to God.

The above account is very encouraging to me. I take full responsibility for the trouble I am in. No one else is to be blamed. I humble myself greatly now before God and ask for His favor, grace and mercy. One point I don't like to think about is that Manasseh spent twelve years in captivity before he was restored. I wonder, "Is this what God means when He says He will restore in due time?"

Journal Entry
November 24, 2001

David has always been one of my biblical heroes. I've just reread the account of his sin with Bathsheba. I was reminded again how he was so blinded by his sinful self-centeredness that he did what he obviously knew was wrong, just to satisfy his desires of the flesh. He did this even though he professed to love the Lord. Once his sin was known and he was confronted, he was filled with remorse and repented. Psalm 51 reflects his cry to the Lord.

"Have mercy upon me, O Lord, according to thy lovingkindness: according unto the multitude of thy tender mercies blot out my transgressions. Wash me thoroughly from mine iniquity, and cleanse me from my sin. For I acknowledge my transgressions: and my sin is ever before me. Against thee, and thee only, have I sinned, and done this evil in thy sight: that thou mightiest be justified when thou speakest, and clear when thou judgest." Psalms 51:1-4

Why did it take getting caught to bring David to his knees? Why didn't he see that his life would have been so much better without the sin? He had everything anyone could want; God called David a man after His own heart.

I think the reason I have always been able to identify with David is because, even though I love the Lord deeply and He has blessed me abundantly, I still have willfully sinned at various times. I have been caught up in that old "sin/repent, sin/repent, sin/repent" cycle throughout life and especially over the past two years. Now I have been found out and, like David, I am flat on my face in repentance. Psalms 51 has become my prayer too.

I realize that there will be consequences, but I pray, like David, to be restored to the joy of His salvation. [Verse 12] I have already committed myself to "teach transgressors thy ways," [Verse 13] no matter what consequence the Lord chooses to allow. I am not trying to bargain with the Lord, but rather to express my desire to serve Him no matter what comes my way. I feel as though I should warn men of the dangers and traps that lie in wait for them, particularly on the Internet. I also want to encourage men to seek the Lord as the only source of joy, peace, and satisfaction in life.

The Day Before Deer Season

November 25, 2001, was the Sunday before the opening day of Pennsylvania deer season. This was like a holiday in our family. For as long as I can remember, years before I was old enough to hunt, I recall the excitement of my dad and grandfather, and eventually my older brothers, as they cleaned their guns and organized all their hunting clothes and boots for the early morning trek into the woods the next day.

Now that I was middle-aged and had two sons and grandsons of my own, nothing had changed. My sons always managed to get off work or out of college to make it home for that opening day. We lived next door to Peggy's sister and family who ran the family farm. Peggy's sister had three sons who were close in age to our sons. As they were growing up the five boys acted more like brothers than cousins. I had been an integral part of getting the three cousins interested in hunting too. One of the cousins had been the one who came down on the infamous morning that the police and FBI came to our house.

On that Sunday evening when the time came for us to start getting our guns cleaned and clothes ready, my youngest son, Mike, asked, “Hey dad! What’s this Jeff tells me about the State Police being her for a couple of hours a few days ago?” I tried to not look surprised or panicked by the question. I said, “Oh, don’t worry about it. You know in my line of work I deal with people with lots of problems. They just had a few questions they wanted to ask me. I’m not supposed to talk about it right now.” Mike asked again, “Well, we aren’t in any danger are we? I don’t want my family here if there is any possibility that there could be anyone trying to hurt someone.” I replied, “No, there is no need for concern, everything is fine now.” That answer ended the conversation for the time being, but I sensed that neither Mike nor our older son, Patrick, were exactly comfortable with my answer.

Opening Day of Deer Season

The next morning we made our traditional trek into the woods before daylight. It had been our habits to have my two sons get into their tree stands, and then mid morning I would start walking around them slowly in the hope of moving some deer in their direction. We had been doing that ever since they were teenagers and I was concerned about them getting lost in the woods. Now that they were in their thirty's it still worked quite well. I was more interested in seeing them be successful in getting a deer than getting one myself.

As I was walking near Patrick's deer stand I noticed that he was climbing down, so I walked over to see if there was something wrong. He said, "Dad, sit down and take a rest." So, we sat down on a log nearby. He asked, "What was this whole thing with the police really about?" I repeated that it was nothing he needed to be concerned about and again that I was not supposed to discuss it with anyone at this point. I said, "There will likely be a time when I can discuss it with you." "Who said you can't discuss it?" he persisted. What was I to say honestly? I suppose I could have just said I'm not going to talk about it, but I have never had that kind of relationship with my sons. We had always been very open about everything.

I decided that I had to tell him at least the highlights of the situation. I started with my childhood abuse and continued up through the problem with the pop-ups on my computer and how I believed that Satan had lured me into a snare with child pornography websites. We cried and prayed together. I asked that he not tell anyone at this point since there was still a chance that the whole thing could get dismissed. However, I said that I would need to tell his brother Michael as soon as possible because I felt terrible keeping it from him.

We separated again for the rest of the day and continued our hunting. As it turned out, there was no time when I could get Mike alone to tell him before he had to head back to his home four hours away. I knew I had to find a time as soon as possible though.

Devastating News from My Attorney

On November 27, 2001, I received a second letter from the U.S. Attorney's office. This one was to inform me that I was entitled to services from the Federal Public Defender if I so desired. I was given the person's name, address and phone number should I choose to use those services. I knew I was planning to use my own private attorney, but the letter only served to remind me again about how serious this situation was going to be.

That same day I met for the second time with our attorney in Elmira. That turned out to be a difficult meeting. He informed me that after doing some research on cases similar to mine he had discovered that it was very likely that what I had done would be considered a violation of Federal law. He handed me a copy of the law that applied to my case and asked me to read it for myself. It clarified what the Federal government considered "possession" as it relates to any material one brings up on the computer screen. It stated that once an image is brought up on a person's screen, that person is in control of it and, therefore, can choose to delete it or place it in a file or even print it out. I had not done any of those things, but according to the law, by the fact that I had the image on my screen I was guilty of possessing it.

This news was further heartbreak for Peggy and me. We had expected that we were going to go into our attorney's office that day and have him tell us that he had found definitive proof that what I had done could not be considered possession. Instead, we heard just the opposite. He also told us that my case would likely go to Federal court in Williamsport. Therefore, he believed that I would be better served by working with an attorney from Pennsylvania who was familiar with the Federal court system. He recommended a person who had been the United States Attorney for the Middle District, but who had recently left that position to return to private practice in Harrisburg, Pennsylvania.

Peggy and the 2001 Christmas Tree

It had become the custom at our house for Peggy and me to go to a local tree farm and cut our Christmas tree on the day after Thanksgiving. Our sons and their families would then come home on Saturday or Sunday in time for the opening day of deer season. Once they were home with their families, Peggy encouraged our sons to help by getting the tree inside and setting it up and the grandkids helped decorate it. This year was no exception.

However, Tuesday of the following week after the boys and their families had returned home, Peggy still needed to put the finishing touches on the tree trimming. I was so depressed that I could not do anything to help. She told me to just sit and watch her, which I did. The Christmas music was playing softly in the background and I sat and cried. The only thing I could think about was the possibility that Peggy might be decorating alone like that for the next several years, if I was incarcerated. My heart ached for her. She did not deserve any of the stress and turmoil she had to endure as a result of my actions. How could I ever thank her enough for standing with me through these trying days?

Meeting with Harrisburg Attorney

On November 30, 2001, three days after my Elmira attorney recommended a new attorney in Harrisburg, Peggy and I traveled through torrential rain to meet with him. He would not allow Peggy to come into his office with me and that made me very uncomfortable. In his office he was accompanied by an assistant who, along with the attorney, sat across the table from me. Once again, for at least the fourth time, I explained my life story and the current legal problem I was experiencing.

I found it extremely frustrating because the attorney kept saying, “Are you sure you’re telling the truth?” He repeated various aspects of what I had told him and said, “Are you absolutely sure you are not lying to me?” I understood that before he could decide whether to take my case he had to be sure about the facts. However, he was very intimidating to me and I wasn’t sure I would be comfortable with him. But then, since he had been the U.S. Attorney he had to be good at his craft and that would only be good for me.

Ultimately, he told me he wasn’t sure if he could do much to defend me. He reminded me that if he decided to take my case he required a $4000.00 retainer up front. He left the room for a few minutes and his assistant stayed with me.

The assistant was reassuring and told me that it might not turn out to be as bad as it sounded. When the attorney came back he told me that he could not decide that day whether to take my case or not. He said the outcome might be rather clear cut and that I should expect to be incarcerated for three to four years. At that point I didn't think I wanted him to be my attorney. It sounded like he was still wearing his U.S. Attorney hat and was not interested in defending me. He told me he would have to get back to me in a few days with his decision.

Once I was able to be back with Peggy I had to tell her everything he had said. It looked very bleak to both of us, although, Peggy in her usual trusting way said we should not underestimate the power of God to change things from what men may predict. She was always optimistic about every situation we had encountered in life. She constantly had reminded me over the years to simply trust the Lord in everything. She was always correct. Her attitude was always to trust that things were not going to turn out as bad as it seemed. My attitude was that no matter how something turns out, I will accept it as God's will and trust that He knows best. Together we made a great team.

We started the three and a half hour trip home through heavy downpours of rain. The weather was a direct reflection of my whole demeanor at that point. I wanted to just keep on driving and somehow run away from this nightmare we were living.

Journal Entry
December 1, 2001

Peggy and I have been in constant prayer for God's mercy. We have read and claimed scripture verses, cried and prayed in the middle of the night. Yesterday, I met with a high powered attorney in Harrisburg. He was not encouraging. In fact, he said he was skeptical that he could do much to change the normal consequences of my actions. It seems that the law is very clear and that to have an illegal image on the computer screen for a millisecond is considered possession. I didn't realize that to only view something without saving it to a file or printing it or allowing anyone else to see it could still be illegal. I visited a free, easily accessible Yahoo website. He said that my actions could lead to me spending three to four years incarcerated and losing nearly everything we own. He was skeptical that he would be able to get the charges reduced. It appears that the FBI had set up certain websites on the Internet to trap people who were interested in viewing their illegal material and I was one who visited one of those sites.

"But every man is tempted, when he is drawn away of his own lust, and enticed. Then when lust hath conceived, it bringeth forth sin: and sin, when it is finished, bringeth forth death." James 1:14-15

I realize that it was actually Satan and his demons who tempted me, not the FBI. I am not blaming or trying to say, "The devil made me do it." I was "drawn away of my own lust" as the scripture says. I was enticed and then hooked and ultimately caught like a fish. Some fish are thrown back to swim another day. Others, especially the "big ones" are prized by their captures. I think I am a "big fish" for the investigators and they likely have no intention of throwing me back. However, we constantly are praying for God's mercy and the opportunity to start fresh without the Internet in my life.

Journal Entry
December 2, 2001

I don't think I have been closer to the Lord than I am right now. I am heartsick, broken and my spirits are low. The waiting, not knowing my destiny, and knowing that it is going to be decided, most likely, by people who don't know Christ, is devastating. I am constantly sick to my stomach. However, I am in continuous prayer, pleading for God's mercy. He promises that after we have been tested He will bring us forth mature. I don't know if that will be next week or after He allows them to incarcerate me for some period, but I know that it is true.

When I envision Christ hanging in agony on the cross, bearing the penalty for my sin, I am again sickened to think that I would selfishly and willfully sin against His great love. Yet, I did and now I am totally repentant. I want to serve Him totally and all other form of work seems so insignificant to me now.

I am aware that Christ may well let me suffer the severest of consequences as part of His maturing and healing work in me. I pray for mercy and that less severe consequences will accomplish the same results in me. In fact, I have made that commitment to God.

Journal Entry:
December 4, 2001

Today the Harrisburg attorney called to let me know that he would not be taking my case, but would refer me to someone else who would be able to provide excellent representation.

He had not been able to reach that person yet, but would keep trying and would let me know as soon as he was able to speak to him.

Journal Entry: December 6, 2001

Meeting with Local Counselor: We met with the local Christian counselor for the second time. We had an excellent session, but at the conclusion he told me that, given the seriousness of the case and the legal aspects intertwined in it, he did not feel as though he could give me what I needed. He gave me a referral to a different Christian counselor located in Williamsport, Pennsylvania whose name is Dr. Timothy Bryant. He had heard Dr. Bryant present at a conference he had attended and had picked up one of his business cards. He was impressed with him and believed that he had the skills to handle my needs.

Phone Call from Harrisburg Attorney: Today the Harrisburg attorney called to tell me that he was referring my case to an attorney in Williamsport. He indicated that he had discussed my case with the Assistant U.S. Attorney and that it appeared that there might be a little room for some negotiation. He indicated that there was some evidence to prove that my case was a little different from some of the others caught in the sting. He had already spoken to the new attorney who would be calling soon.

We truly feel that God is intervening and that He is hearing and responding to our prayers. Both the local counselor and the Harrisburg attorney have referred us to other people, but both are in Williamsport. That will make our traveling much more convenient, plus, I am more comfortable knowing that we will be out of town as we meet with these people, which will protect our privacy a little better.

Additionally, hearing that glimmer of hope that perhaps my case will not be handled in the severe manner in which the Harrisburg attorney had indicated is indeed good news. At least we feel like there is movement in the right direction.

Journal Entry
December 6, 2001
Number Two

"My son, despise not the chastening of the Lord; neither be weary of His correction: For whom the Lord loveth he correcteth; even as a father the son in whom he delighteth." Proverbs 3:11-12

I am writing this now in the evening. When this day started I knew that some important decisions were going to being made today, in Williamsport, which could affect my whole future. The Lord showed me the above verses and I realized that there was likely to be more chastening coming. Now, in the evening I've learned that there is less of a chance of three or four years of incarceration. There is still the threat of some pretty serious stuff though and I will gladly receive the Lord's correction.

"Trust in the Lord with all thine heart; and lean not unto thine own understanding. In all thy ways acknowledge Him, and He shall direct thy paths." Proverbs 3:5-6

Today I knew that two men were meeting to discuss my troubles and that their decisions would affect the rest of my life. I felt totally helpless. However, I know and am very close to another person who has the power and authority to control both of these men. I trusted in the Lord and asked Him to overwhelm these men with His grace and mercy on my behalf. I am prepared to accept whatever the outcome since I know that it will be "of the Lord."

The Lord did show His compassion. Peggy and I feel a deep sense of gratitude and, of course, relief. I have promised the Lord that I will use this experience to minister for Him, and I will. However, it is far from over!

Contact with New Attorney

On December 8, 2001, I had my first phone conversation with my new attorney. In order to preserve his privacy I will refer to him as Mr. Tice. We decided that Peggy and I would go to Williamsport to meet with him the next afternoon, which was Sunday. It seemed strange doing something like that on a Sunday, but we certainly wanted to get the process moving as soon as possible. In my phone conversation he told me some things that were difficult for me to hear. He said he was preparing me for some of the details we would discuss the next day.

He said that, based on what he knew about my case at that point, I should be prepared to have some very negative publicity and would most likely lose my job. That was the very thing I had been telling Peggy I didn't think would happen. He also said that he believed that I would never be able to work in the human service field again once this case became public. I asked if there could be some way of preventing it from becoming public and he said that it would be impossible, since all legal actions in the court are public and available to the news media.

Journal Entry
December 8, 2001

"For in that He died, He died unto sin once: but in that He liveth, he liveth unto God. Likewise reckon ye also yourselves to be dead unto sin, but alive unto god through Jesus Christ our Lord. Let not sin therefore reign in your mortal body, that ye should obey it in the lusts thereof. Neither yield ye your members as instruments of unrighteousness unto sin: but yield yourselves unto God, as those that are alive from the dead, and your members as instruments of righteousness unto God." Romans 6:10-13

I know these verses apply more to my salvation experience. However, they apply also to an admonishment about how I should walk with the Lord in my daily Christian life. I am dead to the sins of my past. I will not yield the members of my body [particularly my mind] to the lusts that have plagued me. I am yielded unto the Lord "as one alive from the dead" and I commit to yield my members as instruments of righteousness unto God.

I pray that by God's grace these will not be just empty words, but rather, will become the actual truth of how I live each day. I pray for God's grace to help me mature and grow so that these verses are unquestionably descriptive of my walk with Christ.

Harsh Truth from My New Attorney

The next day, December 9, 2001, we went to Williamsport to meet Mr. Tice, my new attorney. It was clear that he was part of a prestigious law firm and for that we were grateful. It was also easy to understand that he was very accustomed to working within the Federal court system. He explained that he had experience representing people charged with serious criminal offenses. He mentioned that there was a person on death row whose case he was handling at the time.

He repeated some of the points that he had told me on the telephone the previous day, but it was good that Peggy got to hear them directly from him. He showed us the law books where the statutes were written that pertained to the charge against me. He clarified that the FBI had been able to use special software to restore images that I had deleted from my hard drive.They were, therefore, able to use those as the evidence against me. In reality, they didn't need those because I had admitted visiting the website in question and had signed a confession statement that day in my home when they came to do the search.

Mr. Tice showed us from the law books what the possible sentences could be for the charge leveled against me. It would depend on how many counts of possession they decided to charge me. The issue was whether my whole hard drive would be considered one count or if they would count each individual image on the drive. The answer to that question would totally determine the seriousness of the charge and subsequent sentence. One scenario could lead to the three to four years of incarceration that the Harrisburg attorney told me about, while the second scenario, considering the hard drive as one charge, would be significantly less.

My new attorney explained that his job in representing me was to get the charge reduced down as far as possible and therefore limit the sentence. However, he was quite clear that he did not believe that the case would be thrown out and that I should prepare for some period of incarceration. He said his best hope would be for eighteen to twenty-four months.

Peggy and I were once again devastated. When the Harrisburg attorney had told me that he thought there was room for some negotiation, we thought he meant there was a possibility of having the case dismissed. Now we knew otherwise. We were totally unfamiliar with the workings of the legal system, but we could see we were in for an educational process. My attorney told us that he would be working with the Assistant U.S. Attorney in an effort to get the charge as low as possible and that he would be getting back to us soon.

One of the most frightening statements made by my attorney in that first meeting was when he said, "I will do everything possible to keep you from being incarcerated before Christmas." We had no idea that could even be a possibility at that time. I immediately thought about the fact that our son Michael didn't know anything about it yet. That was going to be difficult since we had agreed it was not something that could be done over the telephone. We knew we had to try to set up a quick visit to his home.

Informing our Pastor

That same evening we decided to stop at the parsonage to tell our pastor and his wife everything that was happening. We wanted them to know, but also that would give us someone else to lean on who would pray for us. I was a deacon in the church and was the teacher of the adult Sunday school class. Pastor Wil and Suzy were shocked, but very compassionate, as we knew they would be. We loved them and now it was comforting to know they were supporting us. I told Pastor that I thought that I should resign my positions at the church. He cautioned me to not get in a hurry about that. He suggested, as did our attorney and first counselor, that we wait. Pastor Wil prayed for us and asked a lot of questions about the legal aspects of the case. We hugged and went home relieved.

First Meeting with Dr. Bryant

On December 11, 2001, Peggy and I traveled to Williamsport to Cornerstone Family Health where we met with Dr. Timothy Bryant for the first time. We were pleased to discover that Cornerstone was a full service medical practice and the counseling was just one component. Furthermore, it was a Christian organization throughout.

We immediately felt comfortable with Dr. Bryant and could see that he was going to be someone with whom we would be able to be very open as we progressed. I asked if he would agree to allow Peggy to be present for all of our sessions. Since I had kept her in the dark about my issues during our whole marriage, I wanted her to know everything from this point forward. He agreed, although he suggested that we might decide that there would be times when I would want to change my mind about that in the future.

Of course, once again I had to start from the beginning to tell my whole life story. It seemed as though every time I told the story to someone who would be interested in the spiritual aspects of my life, the more difficult it was for me to talk about it without a lot of emotion. I knew if Dr. Bryant was going to able to help me, once and for all, deal with the emotional scars that I had carried, I would have to be very detailed and talk about not just what happened, but how it all affected me mentally, emotionally, and spiritually.

As I talked through my life story and then the legal battle that I now faced, I was crying and actually trembling. A typical counseling session is fifty minutes long and it was going to take more than that to just tell my whole story. Dr. Bryant asked if it would be possible for us to stay around Williamsport and return for another session later in the day. I knew I could not do that since my Pathways Board of Directors meeting was scheduled for late that afternoon. He placed a couple of phone calls and changed his next appointment and agreed to see us for a double session that day. That was extremely helpful because it not only gave me a chance to finish telling my story, but it also gave him the opportunity to respond with some thoughts for us to take home and think about before coming back for our next session the following week. We left the double session thankful that we had the opportunity to meet with Dr. Bryant and looked forward to the next session.

After we left Dr. Bryant's office and started the drive back home, I had to shift my thinking to the Board meeting that was coming up in a couple of hours. I loved my job and couldn't help but think about Mr. Tice's comment that I would most likely lose it. His statement that he would try to keep me from being incarcerated before Christmas raced through my mind. I was concerned about Pathways and the potential negative impact this whole situation could have on the organization. But, I had to keep moving forward as though nothing was happening. Throughout life I had learned to put on a mask to appear on the outside different than the way I was really feeling on the inside. That day was no exception.

Journal Entry
December 13, 2001

I am battling a combination of fear, depression, and deep sorrow for or because of my sin. Even though I know God has forgiven me and Peggy is right beside me with remarkable support and faithfulness, the looming potential consequences of my sin are constantly hovering over me. I can relate to David's words in *Psalms 51*, *"my sin is ever before me."* I pray all day long for God to rescue me from my trouble. His mercy is what I pray for again and again.

My heart is broken and I am brought low. I admit that I had become self-centered and sought my own self-satisfaction rather than seeking and pleasing God. In my loneliness and depression I made bad choices in a feeble attempt to make myself feel better. Those choices only served to separate me more from the Lord, the only one who could have lifted me out of the depths I was in.

I am devastated now as I realize that the sexual abuse of my childhood has actually affected me in deep ways, even though I have spent a lifetime denying it. It changes the way I view sex and crippled my ability to be truly intimate. However, Peggy and I have certainly had a beautiful relationship, even though I attribute it more to Peggy than to myself. It is so confusing to me right now. I can see that abusive acts that occurred in my childhood have impacted my thinking and are even now intertwined in my thoughts.

Where do I go from here? I know that I need help. I have heard that what people in my situation need is [1 the Word of God, [2 the Spirit of God, [3 the people of God.

1. Peggy and I are searching and reading the Word daily.
2. I am continuously seeking the Lord and his Holy Spirit to grant me mercy, grace and healing.
3. I have sought the wise counsel of Godly people.

I know that I must seek God wholly with all my being. I reject the selfish attitude and behaviors that led me into this trouble and seek to be totally yielded to the Lord. Sin got me here but total repentance and devotion to Him is the only way back to Him.

God's Intervention

On December 15, 2001, I had a phone conversation with my attorney, Mr. Tice, in which he told me that the Assistant U.S. Attorney indicated that he was in no rush to prosecute my case. He acknowledged that there were differences in my case from the others who had been caught in the FBI sting operation and that he was willing to go slow, since he had other more pressing matters right now.

Journal Entry
December 15, 2001

Waiting: Be still and know that I am God. Wait on the Lord. Trust in the Lord with all thine heart, lean not unto thine own understanding. These are some of the scriptural concepts that are flooding my mind as I wait. My attorney said today to just enjoy the holidays and we will deal with my troubles in January. It was only six days ago that he told me that I might be incarcerated by Christmas. But now, waiting is a mixed blessing. The waiting is extremely difficult, but the reprieve is welcome. It gives more time for me to meet with my counselor, my second son, Michael, and time to continuously bring my petitions to the Lord.

I thought that perhaps 1 Corinthians 10:13 didn't apply here. Now, I see that the reprieve is ensuring that we are not tested beyond our limits to bear. The comments from my attorney sounded like God may be providing the way to escape a terrible repercussion for my sin.

This is the biggest test of my life. I will not fail. By God's grace, I will not fail. I pray that I will mature in Christ and learn what He wants me to learn from this. I pray that this testing will not be wasted.

"Trust in the Lord with all thine heart; and lean not unto thine own understanding. In all thy ways acknowledge Him, and He shall direct thy paths." Proverbs 3:5-6

Trusting: I must revisit these verses. I bring my supplications to the throne of grace all day long. I'm afraid I have not left my worries there, however. I know that this is an indication that I am not trusting that God will favor me with His response. Perhaps it is because I feel I don't deserve a favorable response. Then, I realize that God is full of mercy and grace. I pray for and now trust that He will give me favor that I don't deserve and that He will withhold the punishment that I do deserve.

"Casting all your care upon Him for He careth for you." 1 Peter 5:7

This verse comes to my mind several times per day. I've seen it on a Christian television station, heard it on the radio and in the songs Peggy and I have been singing lately. I believe the Lord is trying to reassure me.

"Rejoice in the Lord always: and again I say, rejoice. Let your moderation be known unto all men. The Lord is at hand. Be careful for nothing; but in everything by prayer and supplication with thanksgiving let your request be made known unto God. And the peace of God, which passeth all understanding, shall keep your hearts and minds through Christ Jesus." Philippians 4:4-7

God is showing me the answer to my fears and anxieties in these verses. I claim them now as precious promises from Him. I know He cares for me and only wants what is best for me and what will bring Him glory.

Journal Entry
December 16, 2001

"Pride goeth before destruction, and an haughty spirit before a fall." Proverbs 16:18

Pride: I have been reminded by someone very close to me that my sin problem involved pride. I can see that now, though I was somewhat blinded to that over the past couple of years. I took things into my own hands rather than turning them over to the Lord. By my own hands I then fed my flesh to try to satisfy my sadness, loneliness and emptiness. Even though I certainly knew that it was the wrong approach, I did it for selfish reasons.

I was frequently overcome with guilt and would repent, only to return to the "pig trough" of sin again later. No matter how many times I repented, I really never broke free from the sin/repent cycle until November 19, 2001 when the Lord intervened, which is what I had actually prayed for. I prayed that He would help me to break free from the terrible trap I was in. Thank you Jesus for setting me free!

The Lord chastens those He loves. This truth from Psalms is now ever on my mind. The Lord is a hard schoolmaster. He is now disciplining me and teaching me hard lessons. I want to be teachable and open to learn what He has for me. I want to be changed in order to become what He wants me to be. I want to be purified just as gold and other precious metals must go through the refiner's fire. I believe that I am about to go through those fires as the laws of man are about to be imposed on me. I pray for God's grace and mercy in this chastising and refining process; but I will accept whatever His will is for me. Psalms 37:24 states that, "*Though he fall, he shall not be utterly cast down…*" I know that promise belongs to me along with Philippians 1:6 which states that, "*He which hath begun a good work in you will be faithful to perform it until the day of Jesus Christ.*"

My Position in Christ

On December 17th we met with my counselor again and, for the first time of many to come, Dr. Bryant challenged me to remember "who I am in Christ". He cautioned me to not let this current experience define me for the rest of my life. That phrase, "who I am in Christ," became a central point in the counseling process of working through my struggles. The following verses are a few of those he shared with me regarding my position in Christ:

Who I am in Christ[2]

Matthew

5:13-14 we are the salt of the earth and the light of the world

John

1:12 children of God

5:24 not condemned

15:1, 5 He is the vine, we are the branches

15:15 friends of God

15:16 chosen by God

Romans

1:7 we are saints

5:1 we are at peace with God

5:17-18 we have the righteousness of Christ

6:1-8 we are dead to sin

6:18 we free from sin

6:22 we have received eternal life

8:1 we are not condemned, but set free

8:14-16 we are children of God, no longer having a spirit of fear

8:17 we are heirs of God

8:31-39 we are more than conquerors

1 Corinthians

1:30 we are in Christ Jesus

2:9 we are blessed by God

2:12 we have the Spirit of God

2:16 we have the mind of Christ

3:16 we are God's temple, His Spirit dwells in us

6:17 we are one with Him in spirit

6:19-20 our body is the temple of the Holy Spirit, we are bought with a price

12:27 we are the body of Christ

2 Corinthians

3:18 we are in His likeness

4:16 we are renewed day by day

5:14-21 we are new creatures, ambassadors, the righteousness of God in Him

6:18 sons and daughters of God

Galatians

2:20 Christ lives in us

3:26, 28 we are the children of God, one in Christ

4:4-7 we are sons, heirs of God

Ephesians

1:1-8, 11 we are chosen, adopted, blessed, have redemption

2:5-7 we are alive in Christ, dead in transgressions

2:18 we have access to the Father through the Holy Spirit

2:19 we are fellow citizens with God's people, members of His family

3:12 we may approach God with freedom and confidence

4:1 we are called with a vocation

4:23, 24 we are created in righteousness and true holiness

Philippians

3:20, 21 we are citizens of heaven, we will be like Him

Colossians

1:12, 13 we are saints with our sins forgiven

1:19-22 we are holy, without blemish, reconciled to Him

1:27 Christ is in us

2:7 we are established in the faith

2:10 we are complete in Christ

2:11 we are free from the power of sinful self

2:12, 13 we are made alive together with Him

3:1-4 our lives are hid with Christ in God

3:12 we are chosen by God

1 Thessalonians

1:4 we are chosen and loved by God

5:5 we are sons of light and not of darkness

2 Timothy

1:7 we have a spirit of power, love, and a sound mind

1:9 we are saved by grace for His own purpose

Hebrews

2:11-17 we are brothers of Christ

4:16 we have grace, confidence and mercy in Christ

8:10 we are His people

1 Peter

1:3-5 we have a new birth, a living inheritance, are kept by His power

2:9, 10 we are a royal priesthood, holy nation, belong to God, have mercy

2:11 we are strangers and pilgrims in this world

5:8 the devil is our adversary

2 Peter

1:4 we are partakers of the divine nature of Christ

1 John

3:1, 2 we are children of God and therefore like Him

4:4 we are greater than the devil

4:9-17 we are in the likeness of Christ

5:4 we are overcomers of the world

5:11, 12, 18 we have eternal life and are safe in God

Revelation

3:21 we have the right to sit with God on the throne

Understanding the truth about who I am in Christ was a significant piece in the process of beginning to accept myself and to overcome the lifelong struggle of feeling "worthless" and just plain bad. Dr. Bryant reminded me to think about the scriptures and to memorize several of them as a quick way to fight against the lie that Satan was continuously trying to get me to believe about myself.

The Days Before that First Christmas

Since I had been informed by my attorney that my case was being placed "on the back burner" until after Christmas and the new year, Peggy and I settled into a little more relaxed position for a few days. We still prayed every day, several times per day, for God to intervene and to dismiss the charge against me if it would be His will. We prayed that God would shield us from public humiliation and financial disaster. We never forgot that God was in complete control and always prayed that His will would be done. However, we also knew that the scriptures tell us that "we have not because we ask not" and that we should "pray fervently" for what we desire from God.

I am sharing the journal entries from those days before Christmas and those immediately after because I believe they reveal more about what was going on in my mind than I could ever relate now a few years later.

Journal Entry: December 17, 2001

One month ago today: It has been one month since the police came to search our home. One month since the Lord answered my prayer and rescued me from the trap of sin that had consumed me. Praise God for His grace and mercy. He has changed me forever. He has shaken me to the very depths of my being. He has drawn me to Himself. He has changed the course of my life. Praise you Father!

I believe I was going down a path that was not going in the direction He wanted me to go. In all of His urging for me to change[*through my conscience*] and His Holy Spirit, I blindly kept walking until, on November 19th, He stopped me, picked me up and placed me on the road of His choosing. After some major "transplant shock," I am now beginning to grow where

He has placed me. His mercy is without equal and His grace is matchless.

Journal Entry
December 19, 2001

Thankful for God's Mercy: I awoke around 4:00 AM this morning and was filled with confusing thoughts. On the one hand, Satan was trying to cause fear and despair to dominate my thinking. On the other hand, God was reminding me of His mercy. I thought about how the Lord showed me His grace and mercy in just the past 24 hours. I was aware that Peggy was awake also. I told her that I was struggling and she suggested that we pray. I was immediately flooded with thanksgiving, not only that we can come boldly to His throne, but also that He had given me such a wonderful mate for life. I told her how blessed I feel to have her beside me.

I got up and went down stairs and turned on the Worship channel on television. Within seconds I saw Isaiah 12:1-2 flash on the screen. It says, *"And in that day thou shalt say, O Lord, I will praise thee: though thou wast angry with me, thine anger is turned away, and thou comfortest me. Behold, God is my salvation; I will trust, and not be afraid: for the Lord Jehovah is my strength and my song; He also is become my salvation."*

I interpret those verses to be applicable to my situation. I believe that my behavior had angered the Lord and He had to deal harshly with me in order to get my attention. I have done all that I know how to do to humble myself beneath the mighty hand of God, as 1 Peter 5:6 admonishes us to do. Now, God is showing His mercy and I can praise Him.

Journal Entry
December 22, 2001

"Likewise, ye younger, submit yourselves unto the elder. Yea, all of you be subject one to another, and be clothed in humility:

for God resisteth the proud, and giveth grace to the humble." 1Peter 5:5

***Younger submit to the elder**:* I have been reading 1 Peter 5:5-11 repeatedly over the past four and a half weeks because it was recommended by the first counselor we went to locally. Unfortunately, I often started with verse 6 because it didn't seem like I needed verse 5. Today, however, it has become clear to me why verse five is also essential as I continue through this maturation in Christ.

The Lord has laid on my heart the concept of establishing a small accountability group of men to assist me in my further development. I have thought of three men who know my whole story and who I respect. All three are my elders, not only in age, but also in terms of their years as Christians. It seems that this concept is in complete sync with verse 5. I want to be submissive to these men so that they can help ensure that I am doing what I need to do to keep my life on track.

Side note: Last night when I first mentioned the accountability group idea to Peggy she seemed visibly concerned. She was concerned that I might share too much in light of what both my attorney and counselor had said regarding not talking about the situation yet. I realized that I had gotten out ahead of her in my thinking and planning. I suddenly panicked and felt alone again. I realized that I must keep her up-to-date on all my thinking and certainly before any action is taken. I need her "on the same page" with me at all times. It is my responsibility to keep her there. It also made me aware of just how vital her support is to me.

Journal Entry
December 23, 2001

Surrounded by Faithful Friends: I praise God for the faithful friends He has placed in our lives. We are blessed with some wonderful men and women who are now aware of my situation and are so encouraging and uplifting to us. Each one has said something like, "I don't think any less of you." All promise to pray for us. What Christ-like attitudes they have. Thank you Father! It is also such a good feeling to know that some of the Godliest people I know are interceding on my behalf. I know that God is hearing many faithful voices being lifted up to plead for His mercy and grace for me.

Journal Entry
December 24, 2001

My Service to God: I have considered the possibility that I should step aside from my adult Sunday school class teaching. I've wondered if I should take myself out of service, at least for awhile or until my accountability partners give their approval to return. However, my wise elders have advised me to "stay the course" and "sit tight" and not change anything at this point. I don't believe I should ignore their counsel, even though I feel guilty continuing.

Today after Sunday school five different people came to me to express their appreciation for the class and complimented my teaching. First, I thank you Father for giving me the gift of teaching. Second, I am going to take the combination of the wise counsel and the kind words from the five members as confirmation to continue on for the present time.

Thank you Lord for the assurance of your love and the confidence I have that you are performing a good work in me through these trying and difficult days.

Journal Entry
December 26, 2001

Reflecting on Christmas Day: Peggy and I spent a restful and relaxing day at home on Christmas day. It was a blessing. I could not help but remember how I had originally been told that I might be incarcerated before Christmas. We talked to Patrick, Michael, and our grandchildren; and we had Peggy's dad for dinner in the late afternoon. We had a fire in the fireplace all day. We spent time together reading the Word and praying together, and individually, numerous times throughout the day. As we knelt together in front of the hearth of the fireplace, the warmth reminded me of God's love. Thank you, Lord, for comforting us. I am so thankful that He gave us assurance of His love by sending His son Jesus into the world to pay the penalty for our sins. Amen!

Two nights ago I was again overwhelmed by the seriousness of the situation. I felt like I was drowning and that no one could help me. Then we prayed on our knees again and the Lord gave me peace and reassurance that He is with me and will never leave me nor forsake me. We have received incredible comfort from His Word. The Psalms have been particularly comforting to both of us.

I do trust and have confidence in the Lord. I know He is in control of the whole situation and will not allow me to be put through more than I can bear, but will provide the way of escape. Praise His name!

Journal Entry:
December 26, 2001
Number Two

Blame versus Responsibility: Over the past week I have been reading about the Nouthetic Christian counseling philosophy, which many believe to be the best approach. It is based on the premise that the Word of God has the answer to all of the problems of mankind. It directs us to look within our "sinful selves" for the reason we have most of the problems we face in life.

I know that the legal problem that I face right now is because of sinful, conscious, bad choices that I made over the past two years. It does no good for me to blame the childhood abuse I experienced for my present day experiences. No one forced me to make the choices I made in the present. I know that I am not at fault for the things that happened to me as a child, but I am responsible for the decisions I've made as an adult, even though they may have been influenced by my childhood experiences.

I confessed and repented of my sinful choices in the present, and I am confident that God has forgiven me, cleansed and restored me to a right relationship with Him. I will not continue to blame my childhood experiences for my present situation. I do, however, need to deal with the childhood issues so that they take their proper place in my past and do not continue to impact my present thought processes. I am hopeful that my counselor will assist me in doing that in the next few weeks.

Journal Entry
December 31, 2001

Last day of 2001: I never would have believed, in my wildest dreams, that 2001 would have brought this situation. When I prayed asking God to rescue me from the trap I felt I was in, I never thought His response would be anything like this. Now as I face 2002 I can't imagine how the Lord will work in resolving my legal problem and how it will impact my job at Pathways. Today we received another letter from my attorney who is somewhat positive, but still talks about serious repercussions. In fact, I am quite nauseous as I write this now.

Peggy and I are praying together two or three times per day and individually even more. We pray that no charges will be brought against me and that there will be no publicity. My attorney's letter states that he is searching for a statute with lesser penalties attached. We will continue to keep up our praying and have asked the few who know to pray similarly.

I trust the Lord and am confident that He is in total control. He has all the power to determine the outcome. He can bring about the results we desire if it is His will, even though in the eyes of man it seems unlikely. I am prepared to accept whatever God's will may be, even if it is not according to my prayer request.

He knows my heart, that I am repentant, remorseful, and totally submissive to His will. He knows that I want to serve Him in whatever capacity He desires. I have asked the Lord to rescue me without the need to totally destroy my testimony, professional reputation, and career. I know that His thoughts and ways are higher than my ways and I accept that He may have other plans for me.

Preparing for the Probability of Incarceration

Since two attorneys had told me that I should expect to be incarcerated for some period of time, anywhere from eighteen to forty-eight months, I thought it wise to prepare for that possibility. I started a notebook with information that I thought Peggy might need to know if I was not home. I included items such as where I kept important tools to where I ordered garden seeds, how to close up our greenhouse and what perennial plants were planted in which gardens. I realized that she already knew most of that information, but it gave me peace to write it down for her.

Also, Peggy and I discussed what to do in case of various problems around the house including what upkeep would need to be done. Of course, one of the biggest concerns was regarding our finances. Since I would have no income, she would likely have to get a job in addition to keeping everything going at home. We knew that our family would always be there to lend a hand, along with many friends. We were sure that Peggy's sister's family, who lived on the farm right next door, would be available in an instant for anything she might need. We also knew that both of our sons would do all they could, even though they lived three to four hours away.

Probably the most serious part of preparing for the probability of incarceration for me was the mental and emotional part. I thought about what it might be like. I feared what might happen to me if other inmates found out why I was there. I even woke up at night with nightmares about it. I would tell Peggy and we would pray against the possibility of incarceration.

I thought about all the major family events I would miss for two to four years, such as our anniversary, birthdays and holidays. Hunting season with my sons and grandsons would not be the same for them. Christmas was always the most joyful and exciting time for our whole family, but it would turn into a sad, devastating time for all of us. I thought that I would be able to handle it, but felt so sorry for the rest of the family. It would cause great harm and pain for them if I were to be incarcerated. That would be the most difficult part for me to bear.

I was committed to accepting whatever God chose to allow. I knew that He loved me and would provide for me. I envisioned myself trying to witness to other inmates about Christ and perhaps even teach a Bible study or counsel others. I was sure I would go through a period of depression, but by God's grace I would survive to bring Him honor.

Chapter 9

WAITING, REFLECTING AND LOOKING FORWARD

Journal Entry
January 1, 2002

Old Year/New Year: Yesterday's Sins and Blunders. When I first awoke this morning, I thought, "What have I got to look forward to in 2002?" What will the Lord lead me into in the coming year? I have to admit that Satan works on my mind making me somewhat fearful and sometimes panicky about the future.

Peggy and I read the *Our Daily Bread* devotional for today. It was one of those times that it was just the encouragement that I needed for the day. There was a quote from Oswald Chambers where he stated: "Our present enjoyment of God's grace is apt to be checked by the memory of yesterday's sins and blunders. But God is the God of our yesterdays and He allows the memory of them in order to turn the past into a ministry... Let the past sleep, but let it sleep on the bosom of Christ. Leave the irreparable past in His hands and step out into the irresistible future with Him."[3]

Amen Lord! I have read these words repeatedly and find them to be an amazing encouragement. I know that I can trust the Lord completely. Nothing will happen that is not within His divine will as long as I am walking closely with Him…and I am.

Thinking Back

At my January 3rd counseling session with Dr. Bryant, he asked me to take some time, at least twice that week, to think back about my sexual abuse in as much detail as I could. I was to think about sights, sounds and even the smells that I could remember. Then I was to think about the feelings I had at the time and compare those to the feelings I was having presently.

The next day, I talked openly about it to Peggy in detail for the first time. It came as quite a shock to her to hear the whole story. We sat on the floor beside the fireplace and she held me and we cried together. It was such a relief for me to know that she knew the details and still accepted me. It had always been my fear that if people knew about it they would reject me in some way.

I had always thought that it was not good to dwell on past distasteful events. I had thought that I should press forward and bury the hurt, since I couldn't change it. However, I came to the understanding that, while I could not change past events, I could change the way they affected me. I realized that I am in control of the present impact. I prayed that as I continued to think through the abuse as my counselor requested, and even wrote down my thoughts and feelings, it would help to resolve my deep-seated emotions associated with it.

Journal Entry
January 5, 2002

"I will say of the Lord, He is my refuge and my fortress: my God; in Him will I trust." Psalms 91:2

Learning to place my trust in the One who is truly in control of all of my circumstances is now my top priority. What good does it do to bring all my supplications to Him all day long if I don't trust or have confidence that He will accomplish all that I ask of Him. The confusing aspect here is that even though I know He has forgiven me, I know that He may also allow the natural consequences for my sin to occur. I wonder about the degree of those consequences. I am already suffering some serious consequences, although they may be minor compared to what is to come. However, it is our constant prayer that, in His infinite mercy, He will see fit to rescue me from my time of trouble and spare me the harsh consequences. I trust that He can and will favor us with His response, and yet I am prepared to accept whatever is His will for me.

Today I expressed to my son, Patrick, that I was feeling as though I was just floating along like a ship without a sail, not knowing where I was going. He reminded me that for as long as he could remember, I had always been in a position where I was in charge and in control of most things around me. He asked me to consider that perhaps God was preparing me to let go of the reins and give control over to Him so that He could lead me in a new direction.

Journal Entry
January 8, 2002

Satan tries to instill fear in me on every occasion he can. If I hear something on the news or read something in the newspaper regarding Internet crime or sex crimes, I begin to be fearful. The fear turns to worry and visions of terrible outcomes to my legal issues. I've even imagined the wording of headlines in the local newspapers citing me. All this is a downward spiral leading to guilt, shame and depression. Then, fatigue sets in and I can barely function.

I feel terrible because all these feelings are in contrast to what Peggy and I have been praying for all day, every day. I ask myself, "Where is my faith?" Satan whispers that it isn't lack of faith, but rather just facing reality. If that were true then it would mean that I'm not trusting God, who is all powerful and able to overrule anything that man might try to do to me. All of this causes me to fall to my knees and give my burden back to Christ and to reaffirm my confidence in Him. I acknowledge that nothing will happen to me that He does not allow.

Informing Our Son Michael

Neither Peggy nor I have a record of the exact date that we traveled to our son Michael's home to tell him and his wife about the whole legal issue. We felt terrible that his brother, Patrick, had known since the opening of deer season and yet he was still in the dark about it. I was afraid he would be as upset that we hadn't told him as he would be about the problem itself. My fears were all for naught. He and his wife, Sue, were extremely compassionate and forgiving. We cried and hugged and throughout the rest of the weekend we discussed various aspects of the situation and agreed that there was no need to tell our two grandsons anything about it at this point. They were four and five years old at the time. We did agree, however, that eventually they should be told, no matter what the outcome. I was relieved that we had completed this important task.

Satan's Attacks

Satan was at the core of all of my turmoil during those early days of this legal situation. He was always accusing me and telling me that I was getting just what I deserved. He would plant ideas in my mind that God would certainly never spare me because my sin and lifelong secret and hypocritical behavior were just too great for Him to forgive. I knew that those were lies straight from Satan himself. Yet while I was in that long waiting period, hearing nothing from my attorney, Satan played tricks with my mind.

There were times when I felt surrounded by Satan's demons. I know that not everyone believes in such beings, but I surely do. During the eighteen to twenty months of my struggle with the Internet, I often sensed something or someone urging me to return to the websites that got me into this horrible problem. I now believe those were Satan's demons luring me into sin.

In James 1:14 God points out that, "*...every man is tempted, when he is drawn away of his own lust, and enticed.*" Satan knows what will entice each one of us. It may be something different for different people. For me, it was the lure to resolve the sexual abuse issues in my life. Unfortunately, I succumbed to Satan's tactics and sought a very unhealthy method. Satan will often choose to attack us when we are in a weakened state because we are more vulnerable to making poor choices.

Early in my counseling I began to see how Satan had attacked me. I was constantly questioning my counselor regarding his opinion about how I could have made such a terrible choice as to visit the website with child pornography. I knew it was morally wrong, but I didn't realize that viewing something on a free website could be illegal. I believe Satan placed the dialogue between men who were suffering from the impact of childhood abuse on the same pages as the images as a lure to get people like me to return again and again.

I developed a chart to demonstrate what I refer to as the Vulnerability Cycle in reference to Satan's tactics. It helps me understand my own behavior and lends a perspective for others as well. This chart appears below.

The Vulnerability Cycle

Any Christian can reach a point of vulnerability leading him to lower his defenses and permit sin to enter his life. If left unchecked this sin will entangle him and pull him down even further, increasing the vulnerability and thus the cycle begins.

Initial Conditions That May Lead to Vulnerability:

Stress – may come from any number of sources, individually determined

Exhaustion/Overwork

Spiritual dryness

Loneliness – feeling alone even when surrounded by people

Prolonged physical illness

Depression – loss of hope for the future

Loss of shock over sin in the world

Personal area of weakness – lust or some other moral issue

Opportunity to indulge in one's area of weakness

Lack of accountability

Results of Giving into Sin:

Entanglement – becoming hooked

Desensitization – what once what shocking seems normal and commonplace

Guilt/Anger

Frustration

Feelings of being out of control

Sin/repent cycle

All the results of sin lead back to the same conditions of vulnerability that were present at the beginning, except now they are more intense. Again, if left unchecked the sin is likely to become greater until God intervenes.

Journal Entry
January 18, 2002

Ten days have passed since I last wrote in this journal. I have been busy practically every night with college teaching and a trip to Michael's. We have heard nothing from the attorney in over ten days and believe that to be a good thing. We are having a two-week interval between counseling appointments. That is the longest since we started. It takes a half day from work each time we go. I would have appreciated going this week though. Peggy and I continue to pray together at least three times a day and individually several more times. We continuously pray that God will control the hearts and minds of those who will be making decisions that will determine the course of the rest of my life, even though we know that it is only God who will decide my future. We pray that He will cause them to decide to not go forward with the prosecution. We know that it may seem impossible with men, but that all things are possible with Christ.

It is so hard to know how to plan for the future as we wait. I don't know if I will have a job or where I will be. I feel as though we should go on and plan things as we normally would, and wise people tell us we should. However, I have a certain reluctance to plan activities too far in advance based on the repercussions that the attorneys have told me I could expect to occur.

Damage to the Cause of Christ

As we continued to wait for something to break on the legal front, I continued to work at Pathways and to teach part-time at Elmira College. Both were jobs that I loved and had poured myself into for years. Although I tried to do my job, it was difficult to keep from thinking about the legal issue hanging over my head every minute of every day. I had always tried to have a positive testimony for Christ in all the positions I had held over the years. I don't think there was any question in the minds of the people who knew me well that I was a Christian and one who was serious about adhering to my faith. I used every opportunity I could to be sure that people saw my convictions without trying to condemn others or push my beliefs too strongly. As I think back now, I wish I had been less concerned about offending people by my faith and more forward at explaining it.

One burning thought that I could not get out of my mind was about the damage that would be done to the cause of Christ if the prosecution went forward and I was publicly humiliated in the news media. I could only imagine how some of those I knew, who had always scoffed at my Christian stance, would laugh and ridicule me once they heard the news and determined that I must have been a lying hypocrite. Those who did not know Christ as their savior would feel reassured that they were no worse than me and probably actually better. Why would they ever want to listen to someone present the gospel and the hope that awaits those who become a believer?

I asked God to forgive me for behavior that caused harm to His gospel message. I felt assured that He forgave me and that He was far superior to any harm that I may have caused. He, in His infinite power, was able to overcome the results of my behavior.

Journal Entry: January 21, 2002

Dealing with Guilt: I have spent much time thinking about my childhood abuse issues—revisiting the "little boy" Bruce, as my counselor requested. He suggested that I try to view the whole situation with the compassion that Christ would have in the situation. I realize now that I am not to blame for the abuse, although I have always thought that I was. I realize that God does not hold me responsible for "participating" in the abusive activities. However, I am responsible for the sins I have committed by visiting the pornographic sites on the Internet, even though I most likely would never have been curious about visiting those sites had the abuse not occurred. Reading on one of the sites about other men who had been abused became a strong draw, even though it still had the images as well. I do not blame anyone else for my bad choices as an adult. I still feel much guilt for those actions. I know that I have been forgiven. My emotions are as much shame as guilt.

Journal Entry
February 10, 2002

I have not written in this journal for nearly three weeks now. It was certainly not for lack of things to write about. Our lives have taken some serious turns and Peggy keeps reminding to write my thoughts in this journal.

We were devastated when we received another letter from my attorney. The content was quite disturbing and seemed to verify that the biggest thing we had been praying against was going to happen anyway. It appears more likely that formal prosecution will go forward. We were clearly shaken and began to wonder if God was going to deny all of our prayer requests in this situation.

A week has now passed since receiving the letter and we are beginning to regain some confidence. We never stopped trusting the Lord, but have had to adjust our thinking somewhat.

Prosecution Likely to Move Forward in Spite of Our Prayers

As noted in the journal entry above, our attorney had informed us that he had received word from the Federal Prosecutor's office that they did not see why they should not move forward with the case at some point. Additionally, he indicated that there would likely be a substantial fine involved in addition to some period of incarceration. We believed we were back to square one and were once again on the downward side of the roller coaster ride. We could never get used to the constant ups and downs that we were experiencing. We felt drained all the time.

Journal Entry
February 12, 2002

Ultimate trust in the Lord: I am trusting the Lord 100% for the outcome of my troubles. I've done all that I know how to do to make myself pure before the Lord. I've given myself wholly over to Him, rededicated my life to Him, and prayed that He will accept me as a living sacrifice. I have given myself to serve Him in any way and in any place He chooses, even in prison if that is His will. I'm asking Him to show me things that I still need to change so that I can be a clean vessel, pure and ready for His service. Of course, I already confessed, repented and requested cleansing and restoration weeks ago. I am studying His word daily and praying continually. Peggy and I still pray together two or three times per day.

Because of all that I mentioned above I am able to totally trust Him. It may sound as though I am trying to win Christ's favor by my works. That clearly is not my intent; I pray that the Lord will see my heart. I want to be in tune with His heart so that He can use me and that I will be able to readily accept whatever His will may be.

I know that He may not give me the desires of my heart or that His methods may be greatly different than what I think about. I know He will give me the desires of His heart and that is truly what I want, even if it causes me pain and loss in the process. It will be for my good and His glory.

He Shall Give Thee the Desires of Thine Heart

Psalm 37 became a real blessing to me during this waiting period and in the months and years that have followed. I gained a new understanding of that Psalm as we discussed one particular verse during one of my counseling sessions. Psalm 37:4 says, *"Delight thyself also in the Lord; and He shall give thee the desires of thine heart."*

I had always misread the verse to suit my desires. I had failed to really think about what was involved in "delighting myself in the Lord." I came to realize that it included being able to accept and love whatever God allows in my life. If I believed that He would not allow anything other than what was good for me and what would bring glory and honor to Him, then why should I worry or complain.

Additionally, the second part of that verse says that He shall give you the desires of your heart. I thought that meant that if I pleased the Lord he would give me whatever I desired. Wrong! My counselor, Dr. Bryant, helped me to see the real intent of that verse. It means what it says. If I delight myself in the Lord, as noted in the previous paragraph, God will place His desires in my heart. Those may not be the same desires I would choose in the flesh, but would be the desires He wants me to have in my heart.

In my case, it could make me desire to suffer for the cause of Christ, even it was in prison. There was no guarantee that was what He desired, but it helped me to understand that by my desiring to delight in the Lord, He would create in me the desires He wanted me to have. That truth gave me incredible peace.

Journal Entry
March 8, 2002

From the Hilltop to the Valley Floor: Almost another month has gone by. During that time we have had moments when we were encouraged and other times when we were in the deep valley. This whole experience has been like a yoyo for 15 weeks now. This week we were initially quite encouraged, but by Thursday evening I was in the midst of my darkest hour since the whole affair began on November 19th.

It now appears that not only will I be incarcerated, but also levied a substantial fine and perhaps be prevented from receiving future federal benefits, which I assume includes Social Security. I've learned that there are other ramifications to a felony charge that I hadn't known. My attorney informed me that I would also lose the right to possess any form of firearm, which means the end to hunting with my sons, grandchildren and brothers.

So, it appears that I could lose my job and be in a position of never being able to work in my lifelong field again. I could lose our retirement savings, our social security and other freedoms. All this has brought me down with my face on the floor and to the realization that God is really all I have and all I need. Everything else is extra and mine only because of God's grace and mercy.

I have been told that brokenness is when one reaches the point where there is nothing left but God. Nothing I have or thought I would have in the future can help me now, except my trust in the Lord. Praise God Peggy still faithfully stands by me. She is truly God's gift to me in my greatest hour of need. Her faithfulness keeps me going on a daily basis.

Journal Entry
March 8, 2002
Number Two

Remembering His Hand of Mercy: As I try to pick myself up once again, the Lord has reminded me of His grace at work in my life. I must now recount some of the vital ways that He has worked over the past 15 weeks:

1. Drawn me closer to Him than ever before.
2. Drawn Peggy and me closer to each other and to Him.
3. Caused us to study and meditate on His Word daily.
4. Caused us to pray together 2-3 times daily.
5. Caused me to examine my life and repent of various things.
6. Increased my trust in Him.
7. Humbled me as my sin was exposed.
8. He has reassured me of His faithfulness.
9. He has helped me be more tolerant of the shortcomings of others.
10. He has shown His mercy by stretching out the time period.
11. I've not been arraigned, arrested or incarcerated.
12. There has been no media attention.
13. He has given us a fantastic Christian counselor.
14. He has given a few praying friends and family.
15. He has provided us with an excellent and capable attorney.
16. He has allowed me to continue to serve at church.
17. He has allowed me to continue my job at Pathways and college.
18. He has caused the few I have told to be compassionate and supportive.

19. He has arranged that the new incoming U.S. attorney is a Christian known and respected by both my attorney and my counselor.
20. He has brought our sons and their wives closer together and closer to us.

Health Problems Intensify

As the weeks and months of the legal situation slowly passed, my health problems appeared to be intensifying. I had numerous falling incidents, mostly at home. My issues with eye-hand coordination were getting severe and I would frequently tip over items at the dinner table as I reached for them. I had a tremor in my right hand that made it difficult to perform various tasks. I remember that one day during a lunch meeting with my Board president, I tipped over a glass of water which ran all over the table in her direction.

My doctor was still pursuing the possibility that I might have multiple sclerosis. [MS] As spring approached I found it increasingly difficult to do the usual work around the yard, greenhouse and garden. Peggy and I kept reading books and articles about MS and we never found anything that discouraged us from believing that it was possible that I had it. We even went to a few MS support group meetings to see what additional information we could learn. The main point that was continuously stressed was how difficult it was to diagnose. For some of the people at the support group it had taken years with no treatment before a diagnosis was finally made and treatment begun.

I was certainly aware that the stress associated with the legal matters could be adding to the intensity of my symptoms. However, there didn't seem to be anything I could do about it at that point in the process.

Major Events in Mid-March 2002

By mid-March some significant events occurred even though the legal situation had not changed much. Peggy and I decided that I should inform the Pathways Board president about the whole legal affair since it seemed certain, according to my attorney, that at some point soon the prosecution would proceed and it would be public information. The Executive Committee of the Board met with me to go over my annual performance evaluation. At the end of the meeting I asked the Board president to stay so I could tell her. Naturally, she was very concerned, not only for the impact on the agency, but for me personally. She suggested that we have the whole Executive Committee meet again so that I could inform them, too. I asked for a little more time since it was uncertain when any legal action would be taken. She agreed for the short term.

During the next few days I had one of my falling episodes in the hallway outside my office at Pathways. The nurse was called and Peggy came and took me home. Within a few more days the Board president contacted me to say that she had decided that it was time to tell the Executive Committee. I agreed, partly because I wasn't sure how much longer I would be able to work due to my health condition, in conjunction with the legal situation.

A few days later, on March 25, 2002, Peggy joined me in a meeting with the Executive Committee. I explained my whole story, including the health issues and the pending legal action against me. They were very sympathetic and concerned. Again, I got the impression that they were as concerned about me as they were for the agency. It was suggested that they consult with the agency attorney to see what, if any, action they should be taking to protect the agency. I agreed that it would be a good idea and informed them that he already knew a great deal about it because I had consulted him weeks ago and he had advised me and referred me to the Harrisburg attorney.

The resultant decision of the Executive Committee after consulting with the agency attorney was that I should immediately take an indeterminate medical leave. As unsavory as that seemed to me on the surface, I was relieved to know that if my situation became public I would already be away from the job. Also, I thought that I would be more able to concentrate on getting help for the physical problems if I was at least temporarily away from work. So, on April 1, 2002 I officially went on medical leave of absence.

Overwhelming Depression Sets In

I had never been so emotionally low as I was during the first few weeks after the medical leave started. There were still very few people with whom we had shared the legal ordeal; that meant there were only a few we could talk to for support. A few of the Executive Committee members kept in touch and some even came to my house to visit. That was encouraging and made me feel as though I was still a part of the organization, even though I think they were coming more for personal reasons.

It was not that I wasn't trusting the Lord, but being home all the time just seemed like a step closer to the time when I might be incarcerated. I had difficulty sleeping and felt like just sitting and staring out the window. I thought about Peggy and our sons and what they must think of a husband and father who would do what I had done. Their support was unwavering, but I was sure they must have deep feelings that I didn't know about.

I had an overwhelming sense of sadness at the thought that my career might be over and my health might be on a fast track toward disability. I had been told that people who contract MS later in life usually deteriorate quickly. I wondered if I did have MS, what effect that might have on a judge's decision to incarcerate me.

I continued to attend regular counseling sessions, with Peggy by my side through each one. I had completed the formal process of dealing with the sexual abuse as much as possible at that point. Our sessions now dealt primarily with seeking help to get through the legal crisis and the horrible impact it was having on us and the possible future events. Another major theme of my counseling was the issue of humiliation and embarrassment. Dr. Bryant exhorted me to be more concerned about what God thought of me rather than the thoughts of others.

Journal Entry
June 3, 2002

Growing in faith: It has been 28 weeks today since our legal situation began. We know that any day, perhaps today, we will hear about the next step in the process. We talk openly about the possibilities that the Lord may allow, but still pray specifically for Him to shield us from the horror of them all. Yet, we are trusting in Him for the outcome.

I have come to a fuller realization that my primary focus must be developing and maintaining the right relationship and daily walk with the Lord. While my reputation is very important to me, it is secondary to my surrender and relationship with the Lord. I know that if my relationship with Him is right and it is my top priority, then I won't have to worry about what "men" think of me. That is in the Lord's hands. What more can I hope for?

I get depressed when I think of the mess I have made of my life and the sadness I have caused for those I love. I can only survive this by placing all of my faith in Christ and concentrating on development of a sincere and pure relationship with Him. Even if I have to share my ordeal with others, it is Christ working through me that I want others to see.

Journal Entry
June 14, 2002

This is the most unusual time of my life. I have a job, but I am not doing it. I have a medical problem, but the doctors cannot diagnose it, so they are treating the symptoms. I know there are some who think that the symptoms are all in my head and related to my legal woes. However, they have been a problem for years, long before the legal situation began.

I am waiting for the legal process to unfold to find out what my future holds. And yet, I know it is all in God's hands. I believe He is doing a major work in my life during this time. There is no question in my mind that the Lord is in all that is happening to me now. I admit that I frequently experience moments of frustration and despair as I wait. However, more frequently, I sense confirmation that He is working in my life and in all the various aspects of the legal process. He has already accomplished some magnificent feats in the legal process that would have seemed impossible a few months ago. Now it is June. Last December, my attorney said that I might be incarcerated by that Christmas.

We know it is possible that it may be months before we know the outcome. We still pray fervently several times each day. We know that our salvation is in the Lord only. I affirm once again that I want to be in the center of His will. I surrender to Him and will be faithful through it all. Satan and his demons try to distract me and pull me down, but my faith and confidence rest with the Lord.

Journal Entry
June 15, 2002

Yesterday Satan tried to distress me by making me think about what a bad person I am. I continuously remember "who I am in Christ" and I thank God for it. Sometimes I speak aloud to Satan when I am alone. I remind him that he is going to spend eternity in the "lake of fire" and I won't be with him.

I seek the Lord quickly and passionately to defeat Satan's attacks on me. I am reminded that if I live in total surrender to the Lord, then the battle belongs to Him. This is, after all, a spiritual battle and God has been fighting this war for thousands of years. I am but a novice, but the Lord is the proven champion who guarantees victory if we trust Him—and I do!

Father's Day 2002

The first Father's Day since the whole legal nightmare started was particularly difficult. I could not imagine what it must be like for my sons to have their father prosecuted for possession of child pornography. They had always been very proud of me for my accomplishments professionally and appreciative for the support their mother and I had always shown to them for their school and church involvement. I could only imagine that they were stunned and didn't know what to think about what was now happening.

I decided that I would write a letter to them for Father's Day to try to express my feelings and attempt to put the whole situation in perspective. I have included a copy of that letter below:

Father's Day
June 16, 2002

Dear Patrick and Michael,

This is my Father's Day letter to you both. I love you deeper and stronger every day. You cannot know how my heart breaks for you. I wish that I could rescue you from every hurt and pain that you feel, especially those that have been caused by my actions. Although I cannot rescue you, I can and will conduct myself in such a way as to make you proud of me once again. I am sorry that I failed you, but thankfully we have a God of forgiveness, and through faith we will endure through this ordeal. My faith has never been stronger.

There is so much about you both that makes me proud and joyful for who you have become as men. Yet, I often wish that I could relive the days of your youth with you. I have fond memories and very few regrets about my role as your father. I do wish I could do some things differently, however, but realize there is no going back to those days.

Now you are fathers yourselves and have the same privileges and opportunities to influence the little lives God has entrusted to you. Frankly, how you and I carry out that responsibility is among the most critical charges we have been given by God. There is no doubt that we will be held accountable by God for the job we do in rearing our children. We will be particularly held responsible for ensuring that they know Christ as their savior and that we prepare them well to cope with this sin-filled world we live in, without getting caught up in all that Satan tries to lure them into.

Your mother and I pray for you, your wives and your children every day, and frankly, sometimes several times per day. We are so thankful for your Godly wives. What a gift from God to have that faithful helpmate beside you every day. It is certainly God's plan that you work as a team, with each of you having a distinct role in influencing and training the children. Never forsake your responsibility as the spiritual head of the household. I believe that duty, given by God, makes you responsible for leading your children to Him. Of course, the best teaching tool is your example, the life you live before them. They must see Christ in you.

I know these past few months have been extremely trying times for you and our whole family. It seems as though your own father has failed to live by the very words that I have spoken about above and all through your lives. I am sure that my current situation must give you cause to question some of the things about the Christian life. For me, these recent events only make me more committed to admonish you to live lives that are pure and pleasing to God. God is doing a very important work in my life right now. I see Him working in various ways every day. I still believe all that I ever tried to teach you from God's word, even though you are aware of my shortcomings and failures. I hope to use the suffering He is allowing me to endure right now as an example for you and others to see that you cannot dabble with sin or lustful, self-centered pleasures that Satan tries to lure us into. More than ever, I have realized the truth of Galatians 6:7-8, "Be not deceived, God is not mocked. Whatsoever a man soweth that shall he also reap." The one who sows to please his sinful nature will reap destruction; the one who sows to please the Spirit, from the Spirit will reap eternal life. [my paraphrase]

I beg you to walk with the Lord every day. Go to Him, seek Him and His will for your life. Only in Christ will we find the peace and contentment we all so desperately want for ourselves and our families. We know that God hates lukewarmness. We cannot play at being a Christian and play with sin or ignore what He commands us to do. We must never be ashamed for people to know that we are Christians or ashamed of our Christian values. He has called us to separate ourselves from the worldliness that Satan offers. I tell you from my own experience that the world offers nothing that will satisfy for very long. Only what comes from Christ will last.

My Father's Day 2002 message to you in a nutshell is to be strong in your faith in Christ Jesus. No matter what happens in our lives, know that nothing can happen that God does not allow. If He allows it, then it must be for our good and His glory. Although we may not understand it at the moment, by our faith we know that it is true. He wants only good for us even though He sometimes has to discipline us in order for that good to be revealed. Do not lose faith no matter what happens. I heard someone say that "happiness should not be dependent on day to day happenings, but rather, lasting joy comes from faith and trust in Jesus Christ." It is that joy that I want for you and your families. Don't just sit back and wait for it, seek it in Christ.

I love you,
Dad

Journal Entry
June 21, 2002

Now we know that the Lord plans to allow my plea agreement to be filed and arraignment will happen soon. It seems that the horror that we have prayed would not happen, may very well be unfolding. We are confused because it seems like so much of what we have prayed against in this legal battle is going to happen in spite of our prayers. I will not lose faith in the Lord. I know He has a better plan for me. What seems like a good outcome to us often falls short of what He has in mind. His ways are higher than our ways.

The Legal Process

I had been totally ignorant of the legal process, as it relates to prosecuting someone, until I was the target. I didn't know that I should not have signed a confession statement when the FBI was at my house on November 19, 2001. I at least should have asked to speak with an attorney first.

I have since been told by an attorney that confession statements seldom end up helping one's case. Yet, I was led to believe by the FBI that doing so would help my case.

I did not understand what arraignment was and how it differed from sentencing, until I had to go through it myself. I discovered that arraignment was when I would be formally requested to plead guilty or not guilty to the charge leveled against me. I was informed that arraignment was the next step in the legal process for me. Now, we awaited word on a date for me to appear. My attorney informed me that there would likely be reporters present and my whole story would be in the news shortly thereafter.

Giving Up my Chevy Tahoe

One of the significant results of my impending arraignment and loss of my job was the realization that I would not be able to keep the 2000 Chevy Tahoe that I had just purchased in the fall of 2001. It had been my dream vehicle for winter driving and towing our camper. I never got to tow the camper with it.

But, the Lord was already way ahead of us in that category as well. One of my Board members at Pathways had been looking for a vehicle similar to the Tahoe and was interested in it. We agreed on a price, and a few days later they took the Tahoe home with them. Based on everything my attorney had told me I had a feeling the Tahoe was not the only thing we were going to lose.

Themes that Ran through My Mind at this Point

Reluctant Journey or Reluctant Traveler

The Fowler's Snare

The Dormant Seed

I was thinking of these themes because they crystallized my thoughts about not only the past 7 months, but of my whole life. However, it had only been during the past 4 months of praying and reading God's Word, coupled with counseling and deep thinking, that I had been able to distill my thoughts down to these major themes. I should say that God had distilled my thoughts until I could see these themes without the contamination of the hustle and bustle of a busy work day.

Reluctant: - to me this meant not really wanting to do something. It may mean you have no choice, but you are reluctant nonetheless.

Reluctant Traveler: - one who is traveling to a destination at which he doesn't really want to arrive. In my case, I have reluctantly traveled down life's road carrying baggage and trying to make the best of it all along the way.

A Reluctant Journey: - This also refers to my life or the life of anyone who has been abused. Sometimes I do not want to move on in life. I want to go back to the little boy I was before, when I was innocent and unharmed, but of course, I cannot. So, I reluctantly move along life's journey, once again carrying the baggage of the abuse. I have forced myself to move on in positive ways. I have tried to prove, if only to myself, that I am an adequate person who has value. This led to doing everything I could to get praise and approval from my parents and all significant people in my life. Fifty years later, I still battle with feeling inferior and the need to be perfect and in control of everything, if not everyone, around me.

The Fowler's Snare: - David makes many references to the fowler's snare or just the snare that his enemies had set for him. I see how this concept applies to me in at least two ways

1. The abuse itself and its psychological impact are snares. I was caught in them when the abuses happened, and have been entangled in them as I have attempted to go through the rest of my life. They have slowed me down, tripped me up and held me back. I cannot avoid or escape from them. They are therefore a part of all I do. Even if it appears to others that I am doing fine, I know that these snares are with me and at any time they could trip me up and make me fall. It is like trying to go through life with a ball and chain dragging from my ankle. Sometimes I can reach down and pick them up and run, but I can only do that for short periods of time.

2. The other application of the snare is really an extension of the first one. Satan takes advantage of my inferiority feelings and tries to deceive me and trip me up at times I least expect it. He capitalizes on my areas of weakness by trying to lure me into his snares as I search for some relief from suffering.

   In my case, I became "hooked" after I saw images on the Internet that were similar to my own childhood abuse, and read, on the same website, entries by men who had been abused as children. Satan enticed me with one image and then my own sinful desires took over. The comments by men who claimed they had been abused interested me. I had never read about any other man who was experiencing the same struggles in adult life as I was going through. All of this seemed to give me some sense of relief, although a poor attempt, I must admit.

I was relieved to realize that lots of other people had done the same things that I had done or had done to me. No one in any of the images I saw appeared to be distressed by what was happening, in fact, just the opposite was true.

Satan tried to sway me into thinking that perhaps I wasn't so bad after all. Perhaps this was just normal, as my first abuser had told me, "This is what buddies do." My older abusers had told me that I was bad and I had believed them all my life. I came to the point of thinking that they must have been wrong, so I continued to visit the website.

All of the above was simply Satan's snare once again. He had dangled the bait that he knew would entice me. Then, my own curiosity and desire to heal myself from lifelong guilt and shame took over and I was caught, and all my shame was magnified. Thus, began the vicious cycle of sinning and repenting.

Trying to Use My Time Wisely

While I continued to wait on the legal process I decided to join the American Association of Christian Counselors. It was an organization that both of my counselors had recommended early in the process. The organization offered books and training courses leading to certification in Christian Counseling. Peggy and I decided it would be a good addition to what I already had been trained to do and would be something constructive to fill my days. The first course was called *Caring For People God's Way*, the second was *Healthy Sexuality* and the third was titled *Breaking Free*. Each course consisted of several training tapes or DVD's with exams for each section.

It turned out that the courses were a good source of mental stimulation for me, particularly because I had been in a serious state of depression. It was reassuring to me to realize that much of the information presented was material that I already knew, either from my formal schooling or on-the-job training.

Chapter 10

ARRAIGNMENT SCHEDULED

My attorney phoned me to report that arraignment had been officially scheduled for July 2, 2002. We had already planned a camping trip with both of our sons and their families to start on July 3rd. We discussed with our family, pastor, and our counselor whether we should still go and it was unanimous that we should continue with our plans.

Now I knew it was time to inform anyone who I believed needed to know before it went public via the news media. I had written a three-page letter a few weeks earlier which I affectionately referred to as the "Friends and Family" letter. I had written it in case the process moved forward and I wanted to inform several people ahead of time or offer it as my explanation after it was public knowledge. I did not send it to anyone ahead of the media coverage, but I did use it as I met with both Peggy's and my immediate families a few days before arraignment.

Informing Families

I contacted my brothers and sister and their spouses and set up a date to meet at my oldest brother's house. I did not tell them what it was about, only that it was critical that they all be there. I'm sure they all thought I was going to tell them I was dying or something of that magnitude. When we met we sat at the kitchen table and I read my three-page letter. Their responses ranged from anger at my abusers to sadness and fear over the possible repercussions legally. I told them that my attorney had warned me there would most likely be some period of incarceration and a fine. We cried and hugged and I promised to keep them informed about what was happening as I knew it.

Then, Peggy and I met with her older sister and her family. These are the ones who live next door. Once again I read the letter. There was also a degree of anger at the abusers and at the legal system. In each family meeting someone asked, "Why doesn't the legal system go after the people who put the illegal material online in the first place?"

Peggy and I knew that there was a lot being done in that area because we had noted it in the news media over the past seven months since we had been tuned into any news dealing with pornography.

We met with Peggy's middle sister and family and again I read the letter. There was not so much anger expressed there, but much compassion and tearful hugging and a promise to be praying.

The general feeling expressed by all three families was shock. I was asked for a copy of the letter by the families so they would be able to share it with extended family members or friends when it was appropriate.

Finally, the most difficult person of the whole family that I had to tell was my father-in-law, Peggy's dad. Everyone in the family was very close to him. His love and compassion and reputation as a peacemaker were well-known. I believed that my story would be a major disappointment to him and his heart would be broken. Furthermore, he was not well at the time. In his case I read some of my letter and talked through portions of it with him. He sat silently as the tears filled his eyes and his face reddened. He finally expressed, "Well, I never thought such a thing would happen in this family." That broke my heart. We cried together and he said he guessed he had better get on his knees everyday over the situation. He was a wonderful prayer warrior and I knew he would do just that.

Peggy's mother and both of my parents had already passed away. For the first time I was glad that they were gone so that they did not have to be hurt by this situation.

Arraignment Day Finally Arrives

It may seem odd, but it was almost a relief when the day finally arrived and I had to appear in court to plead guilty to the charge of one count of possession of child pornography. It was very frustrating because I still did not believe that what I had done should be considered possession. I could not find anyone else who could understand how viewing could be interpreted as possession either. However, my only alternative, which was to plead not guilty and ask for a jury trial, was too risky. One person told me that he believed if you were to ask ten people on the street if they thought that viewing something on the computer screen was considered possessing it, not one would say that it was.

Nevertheless, the time had arrived and it meant that my case was going forward in some manner. I didn't want to hear what sentence the judge might hand down in a few weeks, but I also did not like having my life go by living in this state of limbo. I think Peggy would have preferred that the waiting continue and that we stay sheltered from the negative publicity that was sure to come. I definitely would have preferred that, too, but the choice was not given to me.

We met my attorney outside the courthouse and the first thing he pointed out was that there were two reporters standing nearby waiting to go in. He said any hope of avoiding or delaying publicity was gone. Our oldest son, Patrick, had made the two hour drive to be there with us. We had discouraged him from coming, but he chose to come anyway. My attorney had told me that I didn't even have to come. The law allowed for him to enter my plea. That didn't seem right to me.

The courtroom was an awesome display of wood and indirect lighting. I recognized the two reporters we had seen outside as well as one of the FBI agents who had been at my house. Another gentleman, who I later found out was a person from Federal Probation, sat off to the side with a large folder on his lap. I was feeling particularly shaky that day, my tremor was worse than usual and my legs weak. My attorney and I were directed to approach the rail that was before the judge while the Assistant Federal Prosecutor read the charge against me and even described some of the images they had retrieved from my hard drive. I asked my attorney if I could sit down and he requested that the judge permit that. The judge then asked me if I understood the charge. After responding that I did understand, I also acknowledged that I did not know that what I had done was illegal and that I had not been shown the search warrant until after they had already searched my house and computer. The judge indicated that that would not change anything, since I had signed a statement on the day of the search admitting that I had visited the website in question. The judge asked, "Do I understand that you have a Ph. D.?" I responded, "Yes sir." He shook his head, seemingly in disbelief.

Finally, he asked how I wanted to plead relative to the charge that had been brought against me. I responded, "Guilty." The judge repeated my plea for the record and then indicated that I would be expected to return to the court on September 24, 2002 for sentencing.

Booking

I may not be using the correct term here, but I recall that on the television program several years ago called Hawaii Five-0, the star, Jack Lord, always ended the program by telling his assistant, "Book him Dano," as they hustled off the bad guy to the police station. After the official court action had concluded I was escorted to another part of the building. On my way I passed jail cells and then finally entered a cold room where I had mug shots taken and was fingerprinted. I was then told to go downstairs and report to the Probation Department where I would be given further instructions. If I had any doubt that I was a criminal, I now knew.

On my way to the elevator I met the FBI agent who had been in the courtroom. Unfortunately he got on the elevator with me. It seemed like that was his plan. He confronted me about my comments in the courtroom regarding not being shown the search warrant until after the search. He asked, "What were you trying to do, make me look bad in front of the judge?" I responded that I just wondered if it was an important point. He just shook his head, seemingly disgusted with me.

Once I got downstairs I met Peggy and Patrick waiting in the Probation lobby. I then went in to meet with the person I had been directed to see. He informed me that I would be on what they referred to as "supervised release" until my sentencing date. As he described it, it sounded very much like probation to me. He also gave me a list of the personal documents he needed from me in order to prepare his presentencing report. The list itself was very long and included several pages. Peggy melted into tears when she saw it. She said it would take days to gather everything they were requesting and when they had received it there would be nothing about our lives that would ever be private again. They requested copies of all deeds, bank accounts, insurance policies, vehicle registrations, proof of income with copies of pay stubs and income tax forms along with a projected cash flow statement showing where our funds went. There was still more, but I think you can get the idea. Once it was compiled the documents measured four inches high. Since Peggy does all the bookkeeping in our house and has done so since she quit her outside job when our first child was born, the burden fell on her to compile and organize all of this information. It was just one more way that she had to pay a heavy price for my mistake.

Retirement from Pathways Inc.

On July 2, 2002, late in the evening after coming home from the arraignment, I received a phone call from my Board president informing me that I needed to officially retire immediately so that I would no longer be a Pathways employee as of the next day. Even though I knew full well that that news was coming, it was still a shock to hear it spoken. I couldn't believe my career was going to end this way. It seemed so unfair and yet I had no one to blame but myself. Where could I go from here, when everything I had spent a lifetime developing in terms of integrity, character and a Christian walk, was destroyed in the public's eye by one mistake?

That evening I composed a brief email message to the Board president officially announcing my retirement effective immediately. It was one more loss in a string of losses I had experienced, and I knew there were likely going to be many more in the future. I just prayed that I would not lose my freedom as well.

That evening, after sending the email, I felt intensely depressed and I knew that a long period of grieving was in my future. I knew from counseling people myself that grief does not only come from the death of a loved one, but also from loss of any kind. This legal catastrophe, the loss of my health, and now the loss of my job was like the death of a loved one to me.

Camping Trip the Day after Arraignment

The arraignment was on a Tuesday and we left to meet our sons and families on Wednesday for a family camping trip. Later we found out that my story was told on the evening news that night. During the time we were there, the whole story came out as headlines in two local newspapers at home. Patrick was able to travel to his house, which was nearby, and found the article in an online version of the newspaper. He printed it out and brought it back to camp. At first I didn't want to see it, but eventually I did read it. I could not imagine what people back home must have been thinking. Friends and coworkers as well as other professionals I worked with in the community must have been in shock.

I believe it was God's mercy and grace that led to our having already planned the trip well before we knew about the arraignment. It couldn't have worked out better. We were together as a family at one of the most critical times in our collective lives. We were away from the telephone and well-intended people who would have been stopping in at our house. Thank you Lord!

However, when we got home we still had to face a lot of people who only knew what they had read in the newspaper, which had some serious misinformation. I wanted to write a letter to the editor, but my attorney advised against it. He said that I did not want to do anything that might negatively influence the judge's decision before sentencing. It was very difficult for me to let misinformation stand.

Friends and Family Letter

The following is the transcript of the "Friends and Family" letter that I sent out to nearly 80 people after arraignment and the subsequent news media coverage. It is largely the same letter that I read to our families prior to arraignment, except for the parts that refer to the recent court action.

Dear Friends and Family,

I feel compelled to write to you to share the burden that is on my heart, not only to provide some relief for myself, but also as a warning to you as well. I am currently experiencing the most heart wrenching experience of my life. Suddenly, horrendous events of my childhood, which have sometimes laid dormant and at other times tormented me like a lion chasing its prey, have all surfaced together in the present. Events and thoughts that I have spent most of my life trying to deny or keep secret have become open and public information. I am speaking of the trauma of childhood sexual abuse. Tragically, I experienced two very different episodes of this abuse. One form occurred in a non-violent manner over a period of time when I was a preschooler and the other was a violent form which occurred one time when I was 12 years old. Thankfully, none of my abusers were family members, but were known by my family and me as is so often the case. I never told anyone about my abuse until recently when I shared only minor aspects of it with Peggy. The threats from my abusers silenced my voice and destined me to my own self-imposed prison of guilt and shame.

I can now see how these abusive experiences influenced my life emotionally, physically, and spiritually during my youth and into adulthood, even though I was not always conscious of it at the time. I now understand that migraines, stomach disorders, sleep disturbances, mood swings, the need to be in control, feelings of loneliness and generalized depression [all of which have been a part of my life since adolescence] are a part of a cluster of symptoms related to abuse. There are others also, but too numerous to mention at this time. The guilt and shame had a way of eating away at me until they became the dominating drivers in my life, ultimately affecting all of my thoughts and relationships.

I never sought professional help for my suffering. Instead, I spent my life denying that I was actually hurting and trying to do all that I could to help others who were obviously suffering in some way. My career has been dedicated to an attempt to provide services for children and adults with special needs. In particular, I have helped to establish numerous programs and served on a board whose function was to meet the needs of children who have either been abused or who have perpetrated abuse or both. Since the age of eighteen, when I accepted Christ as my savior, I have sincerely strived to serve God through learning all that I could from His Word, teaching classes at our local church and spending untold hours counseling individuals and couples, along with leading individual and group Bible studies. Most of the people I counseled were involved in some form of sexual immorality such as adultery or pornography. All this time, I was ignoring my own need to effectively deal with the pain resulting from my own past abuse.

Two and a half years ago a series of crises occurred in my life which I now realize made me vulnerable and significantly lowered my defenses. I was the brunt of numerous verbal and written attacks in public meetings, on television and radio as well as in the newspaper, when the agency I head held public meetings to seek approval to open two new homes for special needs children. Within three months of that, my 23 year old niece, who lived next door, was tragically killed in an automobile accident. Two months later I began a severe three-week headache accompanied by dizziness and numbness. An MRI revealed a lesion in the brain, and months of testing began the search for the cause. The result after being examined by specialists, including two at Harvard Medical Center in Boston, is that there appears to be a neurological problem with no specific cure at this time.

During that same period I was teaching an adult Sunday school class at our church. I was requested to do some research on demonology as part of the study. I did a search on the topic on the Internet and found some useful information. However, one of the sites I visited on the topic caused multiple images to open on my computer screen, one on top of another. The images were of all types of animal torture and human nudity. One picture which stayed at the forefront of the screen was of three teenage boys engaged in explicit sexual activity. It seemed like a snapshot of what had happened to me at age 12. I was nauseated and tried to delete all of the images, but each time I deleted one, several more would open. I had to turn off the computer to stop the process. I later discovered that my computer would not restart and it required a technician to repair it. He indicated that I had received a virus from that demonology website.

As the weeks passed, I could not get that image of the three teenage boys out of my mind. It brought back vivid memories of all of my childhood abuse, and I felt traumatized all over again. I also recalled that the image had the name of a website imprinted on it. The name was very easy to recall. Late one night in the depths of depression and exhaustion, I made the mistake of typing in the name of that website and there found several more similar images, along with adult pornography. I was in shock and yet felt a strange sense of guilt release "for a moment" as I realized that others were involved in the same things that had been done to me and yet they did not appear to be distressed. Also, the website contained dialogue between men who said they had been abused as children and they were condemning this site. The moment of relief passed quickly, and intense guilt from viewing the site soon overpowered me. I exited the site and deleted all the history of having visited that site, at least all that I knew how to do. I immediately confessed my sin to the Lord and repented of having ever looked at those images.

Unfortunately, over the next several months, in periods of despair and depression over my own abuse, I was again drawn to the site or others that were referenced on the original site. Each time the pattern was the same. I would visit the site at a time of deep despair; feel some initial sense of relief from guilt, only to be overwhelmed with a new sense of guilt from seeing those images. I would exit and delete any evidence that I had visited the site. I never filed, forwarded, bought or in any way tried to retain the images. I knew that to view those images was morally wrong, but never dreamed that simply viewing and deleting free material on the Internet could be considered possession and therefore a criminal act. I had never heard of such a thing.

Finally, in early November of 2001 I was in total despair from what I refer to as the sin/repent cycle. If I visited one of those sites I would end up crying in anguish over my own abuse and pleading with the Lord to forgive my failure. One night I crawled under my desk and sobbed a prayer that has changed my life forever. I asked the Lord to free me from the draw to view those images or read those comments by others, and to release me from the trap I felt I was in. I again pleaded for forgiveness for my actions. My thought was that I would confide in my wife, Peggy, about this problem and we would discontinue the Internet service and finally I would seek professional help to deal with my own sexual abuse.

However, a few days later, before I had told her, we were confronted with the shock of our lives. We were sitting in front of our living room window at 7:30 AM. We had just finished our morning devotions and prayer when three unmarked cars pulled into our driveway and two State Police cars pulled across the top. Two State Police began to circle our house while a third approached the front carrying a large hammer in his hand. Two others wearing FBI jackets stood in the driveway. I immediately went out to meet them and asked what was going on. The men in the FBI jackets informed me that they had a search warrant and that they were here to search for child pornography. I invited them to come in and told them they could freely search because I knew that there was nothing to be found. After two hours of searching the house plus the garage and basement they themselves concluded that there was nothing to be found. I was never shown the search warrant until they were ready to leave.

Two police searched the house while a third one sat with Peggy. The two FBI agents questioned me in another room and examined all the files on my computer. They still found nothing. I verbally admitted that I had visited sites on the Internet that had the material in question, but never bought, sold, traded, printed or in any way deliberately kept copies of it. I then agreed to write a statement to that effect, thinking I was proving my innocence. I was never informed that simply viewing the images was a criminal act. They took the hard drive from my computer as well as my whole laptop computer. They followed me to my place of employment and removed the hard drive from my computer there as well. A few weeks later I received a copy of the FBI report indicating that they had used high tech methods to restore deleted material and found nothing on my laptop or on my office computer. By this time, I had also been informed by an attorney that even viewing and deleting this material could be considered possession and I could be charged with a felony and be required to serve several months in Federal prison.

It has now been 33 weeks since the five-car caravan pulled into our driveway. Peggy and I have been living in another sort of self-imposed prison ever since. It has been like prison in that all future planning has ceased. Shame and guilt have been magnified and fears about the future sometimes consume me. I have recurring nightmares where I relive my past abuse and envision brutal rape and torture in a prison. I awaken, drenched in sweat and trembling in fright. The only comfort comes when Peggy and I fall to our knees and cry out to the Lord for mercy. We read His Word and claim the promises of His faithfulness, and I yield myself wholly and totally to Him and His will for my life. It is during these times that we experience a great sense of relief.

Since that November morning, I have done my utmost to act responsibly. On the same day as the search I met with our agency attorney for advice. By the next day I was meeting with a counselor to begin dealing with my own sexual abuse. Before the week's end I had the Internet disconnected from our home. Within two weeks more, I had secured agreement from two Christian men to meet with me regularly to serve as accountability partners for my personal and spiritual life. I purchased a replacement hard drive for my computer and had it configured so that it could not be "booted up" until a password had been entered. Only Peggy and a technician at work know the password. I am also working through a home study curriculum produced by the American Association of Christian Counselors to learn how to better help myself and to become a more effective helper of others without becoming caught up in their problems.

The 33 weeks of intensive counseling, with Peggy by my side, have proven to be both excruciatingly painful and abundantly freeing from my lifetime burden of guilt and shame. In fact, even while the

FBI agent was sitting at my desk on November 19th, I was able to thank the Lord, "out loud", for what I viewed as finally freeing me from the trap I felt I was in. As I expressed this to the agent he clearly could not understand. He said that it was likely going to be far from a freeing experience. It was clear we were talking about two different realms of freedom. By the grace of God and the skillful leading of my counselor I have experienced much relief from the clutches of guilt and shame over my childhood abuse. We now deal daily with the realities of the legal system which entangles me and threatens to end life as we know it and have long anticipated it would be at this stage of life. We are confident that we have been led to some of the finest legal, mental health, and spiritual counselors one could hope to receive.

In the weeks of negotiating between my attorney and the US Attorney's office I was left with no alternative but to sign a plea agreement. That agreement makes it clear that the government considers viewing something on the Internet the same as possessing it, as though you had file drawers full of it, which of course, I did not. On July 2, 2002 I had to appear in Federal court in Williamsport to officially make the plea. The alternative of requesting a jury trial and losing would have been much worse as far any sentencing is concerned. I was allowed to be free on my own recognizance, but was scheduled to appear again on September 24th for sentencing. In the meantime, my attorney will be working with the various representatives from government to try to reduce the sentence as much as possible. There are no assurances that it will be reduced. It all rests in the hands of the Federal judge handling the case. However, the information presented to him from the presentencing report is crucial. I could be required to serve several months of incarceration and fined up to $250,000. In regard to the news media, I will only say that as usual, some of the information they printed was not accurate or had been given incorrectly from whoever their sources were.

It is likely that the added stress of this horrendous problem has further complicated my ongoing neurological problems. Since March I have fallen numerous times, have increased pain in my back, hips and legs, along with a tremor in my hand and arm. I have been receiving physical therapy which has provided some relief. I am currently using a cane for walking which has reduced the number of falling incidences. For this reason, the Pathways' Board of Directors approved a medical leave for me which commenced on April 1, 2002. However, since I had to plead guilty to the charge on July 2, 2002, I gave my retirement notice the same day in order to protect the agency as much as possible.

Our faith in the Lord could not be stronger. Peggy and I spend hours in prayer and studying God's Word. We are not simply trying, by our works, to convince the Lord to release us from the legal chains. We are seeking His leading and assurance that, no matter what He may allow to happen from this point forward, He will be with us and guide us so that we can be used by Him to reach out to others who may be suffering from wounds of sexual abuse. Of course, freedom from the threat of prosecution, incarceration, and financial ruin are also part of our prayers, but we have placed that burden upon the Lord as He has commanded us to do. We are prepared to accept His will and yet pray for His grace and mercy. I pray for your patience and understanding and urge you to keep us in your prayers. Finally, I encourage you to seek help immediately if you too, are tormented by the pain and scars of childhood sexual abuse.

Sincerely,
Bruce Hughes

Chapter 11

MY WILDERNESS EXPERIENCE

The Aftermath of Arraignment

Moses spent 40 years in the desert wilderness until God called him for a specific purpose, leading the Israelites out of Egypt. I wonder if he thought that the wilderness was the only life he was ever going to know again. There is no doubt in my mind that God was preparing him to become the person He wanted him to be in order to serve Him better.

The Israelites also wandered in the wilderness for 40 years after they left Egypt and before they entered the Promised Land. They, too, had lessons to learn before they were ready to enter the place God had prepared for them.

I believe that the Lord also provided a wilderness-like experience for me as I had to adjust to His plan for my life. I was faced with a major crisis and needed time to refocus and become willing to do what He wanted me to do. The waiting and the uncertainty for a few years did have a way of changing me. Fortunately, it brought me closer to Him and melted my prideful will into His.

Grieving My Loss and Adjusting to My New Status

Although I had said that in some ways I was happy that my case was moving forward, I was now realizing the amazing difference between being home because I was on medical leave and being home because I had to retire early as the result of a legal problem. The embarrassment and humiliation were tremendous. I did not want to go outside the house for days. Before I would dare go to the mailbox I would listen from the porch to be sure no cars were coming and then hurry out and quickly back again.

I certainly did not want to go to any of the local businesses in our small town. I knew that people had wrong information about my case, but I didn't want to be in the position of having to defend myself all the time. Besides,

I wasn't sure people would want me around them or, especially, their children.

What a difference a day makes. One day I am a respected member of the community and the next day people are distrustful and full of concern about whether it is safe to be around me. I was viewed as a hypocrite at the very least by some. One neighbor told our pastor that their children would never be allowed to attend our church again as long as I attended there.

One of the things I missed the most was contact with people from Pathways and from the professional community. I was active in the communities where Pathways operated programs and participated in numerous functions in support of those communities. Now I was cut off from those people and I could only imagine what they were thinking about me. Again, I was afraid to go into the community because I didn't want to run into any of them.

Someone at Pathways decided that I should not have any contact with any of the staff there. I was told that the door locks had been changed so I could not enter the building and the computer system was configured in such a way as to reject any email messages I tried to send to my friends there.

A few weeks after my arraignment, I met the spouse of one the Pathways managers at a business near the Mall. That person told me that his wife wanted desperately to contact me, but she had been advised that it would be better not to do that. I guess I can understand, and I agree with those decisions if they helped insulate the agency I loved from further harm.

The final blow that had to be accomplished was done on Saturday, July 13, 2002. Peggy and I met the Board president and the Human Resources Director at the Pathways administrative office area. I cleaned out my personal belongings and turned in my keys. It was like throwing the funeral flowers on the grave and driving away from the cemetery. I guess I was feeling bitter because of being cut off from communication with the people who were not only my co-workers, but my friends.

Excellent Treatment by Pathways Board

Now that I have stated my sentiments about feeling cut off from communication with Pathways employees, I must hasten to add that several Board members continued to maintain contact. An excellent and fair severance package was presented to me that made the transition bearable. The package was generous and made me feel appreciated for the seventeen and a half years of my life that I had given working with others in the process of building the agency into a highly successful and respected entity in several counties.

Newspaper Coverage Continued

Sadly, during the next few months after the initial news media coverage, there were at least five more times that there were follow-up articles or that my name was mentioned at the end of another article about someone else who had been arrested for possession of child pornography. In every one of the cases that Peggy and I read about after the beginning of my ordeal, the individual involved actually had hard copies or computer files of images. It is easy to understand that most people thought that I also had hard copies, since none of the news articles clarified that mine had to be retrieved from deleted information on my hard drive using specialized FBI software. At no time did they ever indicate that no images were found in the search of my house. I'm sure that a certain number of people thought that there must have been pornographic images discovered in the house, particularly since I couldn't find anyone who knew that simply viewing on the computer screen was considered possession. When the truth started to leak out there were people who said, "I don't believe it, there must be more to it than just viewing. You wouldn't be prosecuted for that." That's what I had thought, too.

Our Local Church and the Spiritual Community

Peggy and I are members of a small country church. We have both been active in that church for most of our lives. On the Sunday of the headline spread about me in the newspaper we were on our preplanned camping trip with our family. Our pastor handled it very well. He acknowledged the article from the pulpit and reminded people that, as they already knew, things were not always as they seem in the newspaper. He reminded the congregation that they all knew me well and should give me the benefit of the doubt. He urged them to pray for me and our whole family. Additionally, he assured the congregation that he was sure that I would speak about it when the time was right.

Since our pastor had known about the potential prosecution, he had been asking the congregation for the previous few months to pray for a miracle for someone in the church. He never divulged any other information than that. I know people were praying though. At our weekly prayer meeting there was always prayer for the miracle that only God and the person needing it knew about. I truly believe that those prayers made a difference, although you may not understand how at this point.

The following Sunday Peggy and I were in attendance at church. I had discussed with the pastor during the week the possibility of my standing before the congregation to ask for their forgiveness and to give a brief explanation of what had actually occurred. He was in agreement. When Sunday morning came I was more than a little apprehensive about what kind of response I would get. That feeling quickly disappeared though when people started coming through the door. Many came to me, with Peggy at my side, to give us hugs and tell us they were praying for us. They didn't even know the truth yet.

When the time came, Peggy and I stood behind the pulpit, and I asked the congregation for forgiveness for letting them down and for the fact that one of the news articles actually mentioned our church by name. I explained that I knew the Lord had already forgiven me and that I cherished their prayers now for a positive solution to the legal problem. I then gave some explanation about my abuse and its impact and how I happened across the image in the first place. I cautioned everyone to be careful themselves and for their children as they surf the Internet. I explained that, although it is a wonderful tool, it is a playground for Satan.

When I was finished, our pastor asked the congregation to form a circle around the outside of the pews and to hold hands while my father-in-law choked out a prayer for me and my family. When he finished, people were invited to come up and greet us if they chose to do so. The majority of people did come up to us and hugged and cried with us.

The church family became my support group. I couldn't wait to get there each week. I had had little contact with anyone else outside of family for months. I never felt rejected by anyone at our church. Praise God for His mercy once again.

Blessed by Great Friends

During the months of July and August I was pleased that many friends stopped by the house, called on the phone or wrote cards and letters. I even heard from four of the people I used to work with at Elmira Psychiatric Center thirty years earlier. I did start to get some contact from a few people at Pathways who told me that they were not forbidden to have contact with me, but it was strongly suggested that they not do so at this time. One person told me that I was better off not talking to some of the people I worked closely with because "these people are not your friends." That was alright with me. Everyone had to do what they thought was right for themselves.

Of course, as noted above, the church family kept giving and giving of their love and prayers. I heard from people we knew in other local churches as well. I was told that I was on the prayer lists of at least three other churches. Missionaries in foreign countries assured me that they were praying and had the local Christians in those countries praying for me also. God's throne was being bombarded with prayer on my behalf.

Counseling Continues

Through all of the above happenings my counseling continued with Dr. Bryant in Williamsport. I was pleased that when the judge indicated that I had to be in counseling while I waited for sentencing he agreed that I could stay with Dr. Bryant. During our therapy sessions Dr. Bryant helped me make decisions about all the events that were coming at me in the legal process. He never said, "You should do _____ or

_____." He just helped me to see my options and then let me decide how to handle things.

In a later chapter, I will describe the process that I experienced in the counseling and how I came to see myself in a different light. I learned to view the whole abuse situation and the legal problems in a manner that allowed me to move on in life stronger, wiser and closer to the Lord.

Journal Entry
August 3, 2002

I find it ironic that the early childhood experiences I had that were the driving forces in my choice of professional career ended up being the same forces that ruined it. I spent my career trying to help troubled youth by working in special programs and then, ultimately, as an administrator who helped establish programs for emotionally disturbed kids. Many of the programs I helped establish incorporated services for kids who had a history of sexual abuse. It was my way of coping with my past experiences. I viewed it as my therapy and thought that the more I was involved with the provision of that type of service, the better off I would be.

Meeting with Probation and My Attorney

I was scheduled to meet with the Intake person at Federal Probation in Williamsport, along with my attorney, to assist in the preparation of the presentencing report. When I arrived my attorney said that we were not going to meet because he had learned that other people in the country, who were also caught in the same FBI sting as I, were challenging the validity of the search warrants and some judges were granting continuances of the cases until the facts could be ascertained and decisions made.

My attorney suggested that we, too, seek a continuance and wait to see what the outcomes were from the other cases. That sounded good to me. When we left the Probation Office, Mr. Tice told me he would take care of the paperwork to the judge and get back to me. He phoned me a few days later to tell me that the Federal Prosecutor's Office was agreeable to the continuance. That was essential to getting the judge to agree also. On August 13, 2002, I received the official letter from my attorney indicating that an indefinite continuance had been granted by the judge regarding my case.

My attorney informed me that the best that could happen would be that the search warrants be found invalid and, therefore, the evidence would have to be thrown out. The FBI would then have no case against me. Of course, that became our prayer from that point forward. He also told me that he had seen cases stay in the indefinite continuance stage for years before any decision was made. Now we were back in the limbo state, but not complaining because we had been just five weeks away from sentencing.

Journal Entry
August 29, 2002

Yesterday and today I received a visit from my long time friend Matt. We have been best friends since junior high school days. He is the friend I went to New York City with at age 17. It was great to see him again. He had moved to another state and we could no longer get together every weekend as we used to do in the early years of our married lives. We spent one day visiting all the old places we used to go as high school guys. We went to Hills Creek State Park where we enjoyed the lake and he recounted great fishing stories with his father-in-law. Sometimes we just sat in the car and talked. I felt the need to tell him about things in my past that I had kept secret. He expressed his wish that I would have told him sooner and said, "I thought we shared all our secrets." I responded by saying that I was afraid of losing his friendship. I really appreciated the fact that he took the time to be with me in my time of need.

Dinner with the Executive Committee

In late August, Peggy and I were invited to have dinner with the Executive Committee of the Pathways' Board of Directors. These were some of my closest associates from the Board. Most of them had been there for several years and our working relationship was excellent. I had an opportunity to talk a little about my years at the agency and heard some much appreciated praise from the Committee members. They asked for an update on the legal status and again expressed shock and anger that I was prosecuted for viewing and accused of possession, even though I never had hard copies.

They presented me with a wall plague with words expressing appreciation for seventeen and a half years of service to the agency. The evening was far different than would have likely happened if I had retired under normal circumstances. However, I was pleased that they were willing to have the dinner and truly did feel appreciated. Their compassion for Peggy and me was obvious.

Finally, I expressed my sadness that I had not had any contact with the people with whom I had worked every day for years. I told them that I could not imagine myself shunning one of them if the situation were reversed. One of the Board members said, "That's because that is the type of person you are, everyone is different. It may be better this way." I wasn't sure I actually understood that answer, but decided to let it go.

People Still Place Trust in My Abilities

In spite of all the publicity about me there were still people who trusted my judgment and who wanted to come to me for counseling. One gentleman called to set up an appointment with me and I asked if he knew about my legal situation. His response was, "Yes, that is exactly why I want to meet with you, because I know you won't condemn me for my mistakes."

Two other people contacted me to ask for advice indicating that they, too, had been abused as children and had never done anything about it, but were still haunted by it. I even had pastors ask me for advice on how to recognize when someone in their congregation may be struggling with pornography.

I was encouraged by these types of contacts because they gave me confirmation that, no matter how the Lord allowed the legal matter to be resolved, there may be a way I can be used for His glory. I was reminded of 2 Corinthians 1:3, 4 where the Word says, "*Blessed be God, even the Father of our Lord Jesus Christ, the Father of mercies, and the God of all comfort; Who comfortest us all in our tribulation, that we may be able to comfort them which are in trouble, by the comfort wherewith we ourselves are comforted of God.*"

Continued Grieving Process and the Progression of Health Problems

I know that throughout the late summer and early fall of 2002 I was grieving my losses. I constantly felt angry and depressed. Sometimes I was so depressed that I did not want to talk to anyone. Other times I was so angry that I yelled at the very person I needed most and who stood by me day and night, Peggy. She never deserved any of it.

When the first day of school came in early September, I was sitting behind our house on the patio when I heard the school bus go by. Suddenly I was filled with rage as I realized that for the first time in my life, since I started first grade, I wasn't involved in anything that had to do with school and I never would be again. I was plagued with thoughts about how this was so unfair. I walked further out into the back yard where I found a limb that had fallen and picked it up and began beating the trunk of a tree. I partly screamed and partly growled. I continued until the limb broke and I was exhausted. It occurred to me that this was not my normal method of showing anger, but perhaps it wasn't all bad.

I continued to have many problems with falling and tremors. I always used the cane when outside since that is where most of the falls occurred. I still felt like even the grass tripped me up. I was getting physical therapy three times per week in Corning. It did seem to help, but did not resolve anything.

Journal Entry
September 24, 2002

Today was the date that was established for my sentencing back in July, at my arraignment. However, that has been placed on "indefinite continuance," and so we wait. All the waiting seems to place certain aspects of life on hold as well. It is difficult to think about getting a job when I am not sure how long I will be available to work. It could be just a few more weeks or it could be months or even years, according to my attorney. We pray that there will be no incarceration and therefore I will be available for work.

Peggy just showed me an article in the Elmira newspaper. It was the headline of the local section. It stated that my sentencing had been delayed. It was pretty humiliating since it recounted everything that had been in the headline story during the summer and used the words "child porn" in the headline. That was one more hurdle that I had actually expected, but hoped would not occur.

We know that whenever the final decision about sentencing is made that it will all be in the news again. It feels like layer upon layer of humiliation and insult, mentally and emotionally. If I had been employed somewhere, I can only imagine how humiliating it would have been to go to work today.

We will be going to an attorney in Wellsboro for the closing on our mortgage refinancing today. I wonder if that attorney will realize that I am the one written about in today's newspaper. I want to hide, but I realize I must go on. I know, as always, that God is in charge of what happens, minute by minute. I place all my faith and trust in Him. I know that He will see us through. We pray that we will be a testimony to others through it all.

Journal Entry
September 25, 2002

I think I handled the fact that I was the subject of the news yesterday much better than I did two and a half months ago when it broke publicly for the first time. However, I am not looking forward to going to physical therapy today in Corning. I am concerned that others I have come to know there may have read about me and now know about it for the first time. I wouldn't listen to the local news on television because I didn't want to take the risk of hearing it reported.

Journal Entry
September 25, 2002
Number Two

I have thought about how the effects of childhood sexual abuse have chased me all through life; how I ran forward trying to achieve and serve others. As long as I was being a helper of people I was able to keep ahead of the "lion" or the "monster" I thought was following me, which was facing and dealing with my past. However, whenever I slowed down, I felt as though the lion was catching up with me or lurking around some corner waiting to overtake me.

Over the past three or four years I became weary of trying to keep ahead of the lion and became very depressed for periods of time. I reached a point during most of 2001 when I felt I was in hand-to-hand combat with the lion on almost a daily basis. I believe that was because I was struggling with the Internet images and wrestling with the devil. I think I was about to be completely overtaken when the Lord rescued me dramatically through the FBI sting.

I think the sting was actually a demonstration of the Lord's love for me. He lifted me out of the corner where I felt trapped and put me on the road to recovery. I feel as though the demons have been caged and, although they cannot get to me now, they are pacing and licking their lips, waiting for the opportunity to escape and come after me once again.

The Impact of the Legal System on My Life

Hunting: Early October always brings the onset of Pennsylvania deer archery season. My sons and I were avid hunters and always looked forward to those warm, sunny October days when we would sneak into the woods early and sit in our tree stands. We had small radios for communicating with one another, so even if we sat for hours we never felt alone.

Mr. Tice, my attorney, had told me from the day of my arraignment in July, that since my "crime" was considered a felony, I could no longer possess any type of firearm or dangerous weapon. Therefore, I had given my guns to my sons and stored my bow at another person's house. As I discussed the situation with the person I was meeting with at Federal Probation there seemed to be some question about whether I was allowed to keep the bow. He suggested, and I agreed, that since it was unclear, I should err on the side of caution and get it out of my house, for the time being anyway. There is a $5000 fine and an automatic imprisonment for five years for violating the weapon possession law.

Archery season began and I stayed at home while my sons went out alone. My eyes were filled with tears as I stood near our living room window at six in the morning and watched them pull out of our driveway leaving me behind. I later found out that they had had the same eye problem that morning too. It was a long and lonely day for each of us.

I was really dreading the opening day that would soon be coming for deer rifle season on the first Monday after Thanksgiving. That was such a longstanding tradition in my family and I could not imagine that I would never be able to participate again.

I had been having such a terrible time walking and falling that the whole family agreed that it was best that I couldn't go out hunting until I had shown some improvement. The problem was that I wasn't getting any better at that time.

Voting: I had not missed an opportunity to vote in the Primaries in the Spring or the General election in the fall for many years. Now, another repercussion I was told I must endure was that I could no longer vote. I felt like a non-citizen. I couldn't participate with my sons in the sport we all so loved and I couldn't be involved as a citizen to exercise what had always been my right to vote. My attorney told me that those were rights that I had to give up when I pled guilty to the charge against me.

Depression

I felt guilty being so depressed. I thought that if I was truly trusting God as I said I was, then I should be able to live cheerfully every day, expecting Him to take care of me. I did trust Him to ultimately take care of me, but I think it was because of the long protracted process and the fact that I had to stand by and watch life pass me by that I often felt very sad and sometimes stared and cried.

I tried to keep busy and friends helped in that area. Occasionally, some of them invited me to do things with them or came to visit. I was taking the training course from the American Association of Christian Counselors and found that to be helpful and occupied some of my time.

I had spent most of my life feeling worthless, but my counselor had helped me to move beyond that concept. Now, with no job, and no possibility of one, and the seemingly endless waiting to see what would happen in the legal process, I felt useless. Peggy had taken over nearly the entire outside work that I thought I should be doing. However, due to the falling and weakness in my back and legs, there wasn't much I could do. Sitting inside and watching her do all the physical work was embarrassing and humiliating to me.

I discussed these feelings in my counseling sessions with Dr. Bryant and he rightfully referred me to scriptures that extolled the virtues of learning to "wait on the Lord." He constantly reminded me to remember "Who I am in Christ." Perhaps most importantly, he reminded me that Satan was trying to wear me down and ultimately make my life miserable. He demonstrated how I needed to speak directly to Satan or his demons that were tormenting me and tell them that I saw what they were doing and proclaim that I was not going to fall for their tactics to destroy me. He encouraged me to continue in constructive activities such as the coursework and to spend time in God's Word daily.

Peggy and I Hold Special Service at Church

In November, 2002, Peggy and I held a special singing and speaking service at our church on a Sunday afternoon. We wanted to give our testimonies about how God had brought us through this difficulty thus far and that we were not bitter or angry, but rather trusting and open to whatever God may will for me.

We were so pleased that all of our siblings and their spouses were there, as well as Peggy's dad. Many family friends and even three of my former Pathways Board members blessed us by coming. Our theme for the songs we chose and the scriptures we shared centered around "When the Storm Passes Over." Peggy sang a solo titled, "It Won't Rain Always." I was able to share a little about our trust in the Lord no matter what He allowed as the conclusion to the legal issue. Sixty people were in attendance and we felt privileged to have the opportunity to serve the Lord in that manner.

If God allows, I am willing to travel to speak about my life experience and testify about God's faithfulness to Peggy and me through it all. I am yielded to Him about that idea and will continually seek his desire for me.

Journal Entry
December 2, 2002

I can't help but praise the Lord that now we are approaching the second Christmas since the FBI search. I had been told that I might be incarcerated last year. God is good. However, I still live with the reality that a decision about my case could come any day.

Patrick and Michael were here for deer season and once again they brought in the Christmas tree that Peggy and I had cut a few days earlier. Actually, Peggy cut the tree and dragged it to the car. I only offered moral support and held on to my cane. Watching the boys again reminded me that they might be doing that for a few years depending on how the judge rules in my case. I felt like a spectator watching from the sidelines.

The "Up's and Down's" Continue

Hunting again: During the pre-Christmas season there were many up's and down's we experienced. I had talked to the person assigned to monitor me from Federal Probation in Williamsport about the possibility of going to the woods and sitting in my truck and listening to my sons talking on the radios during the opening day of deer season. He said that was another gray area. There was a possibility that someone from the Game Commission might construe my presence as assisting with the hunt and then there could be trouble.

On the morning of the opening day we all got up and Peggy fixed breakfast as usual. However, we were all pretty quiet. Then, the boys left; again I stayed behind. I was so thankful for my oldest brother, Carl, who always hunted with us on opening day. He had told me that he had made sure that the boys' tree stands were ready and safe. He also said he would stay in touch with them all day long so I need not worry about them. Our sons loved and respected their Uncle Carl's abilities in the woods, and I was confident that he would follow through just as he said he would.

When Patrick and Michael returned home they verified that Carl had talked to them on the radios several times during the day. It really helped to ease the pain for me and I'm sure it did for them as well.

Holiday Related Issues: I finally agreed to go out Christmas shopping with Peggy in our local area in 2002. As expected, we ran into people I knew, either from my teaching at Elmira College or through my association at Pathways. One was an employee of Pathways and one was a Corning principal. Neither one would speak to me. However, we also ran into two people from the United Way office who were very friendly and acted as though nothing was any different than ever. I was pleased about that.

We received a Christmas card from my attorney and in it he placed a note indicating that he believed that my case was on the back burner as far as the Federal Prosecutor was concerned. That meant no resolution soon, but it also meant we could relax through the holidays again.

Support from former co-worker: I received a phone call from someone who I had worked with twenty years earlier at Elmira Psychiatric Center. He told me that he followed my career over the years and was 100% behind me. He indicated that he had gotten so disgusted with the coverage in the local newspaper that he called them to complain. He said he thought they had gone far beyond reporting and were engaged in character assassination. It was wonderful to receive such support from someone I highly respected.

Invitation to Snell Farm Dinner: In early January of 2003, I was contacted by Ross Perry, personal friend, Pathways Board member and current Executive Director of Snell Farm, a residential treatment center for court-placed juveniles. I, too, had served for ten years on that Board with Ross until I resigned due to the legal issue. He called to invite me to attend a dinner being held by the organization. I knew that I would feel awkward there, but still welcomed the opportunity to get back into circulation. Snell Farm is a Christian organization where I had been the president of the Board and thus had many friends among the Board and staff. Peggy and I went to the dinner and found it to be a very rewarding evening. It bolstered my attitude and outlook a lot.

Special Friends Treat Us: We were blessed by two couples who were special friends. Each of the wives were nurses I had worked with at Elmira Psychiatric Center. Bob and Joanne Beard contacted us and set up a time for us to meet them for dinner at the Country Cupboard in Lewisburg, Pa.

That was a favorite meeting place for the four of us prior to the legal situation. It was about half way between their house and ours. They lived about three hours away and yet Bob had read about me in their local paper. They treated us to dinner and that became the first of several trips there to meet them. They were major encouragers and urged me to write a book about my life experiences.

Larry and Bonnie Hollenbeck, long time friends came to visit. Bonnie and I had worked closely in the Children's Unit at Elmira Psychiatric Center. The fellowship was wonderful, but beyond that they brought bags and bags of groceries. Bonnie proceeded to fix a fantastic dinner. When they left they gave us enough food to last for days. God provides for our every need. We felt loved and accepted by both of these couples and it meant a lot to both of us.

Employment at Greenhouses

Within six weeks after all of my benefits from Pathways ran out and we had to start paying a substantial amount each month for health insurance, the Lord handed me an opportunity. My sister-in-law Ellen, Carl's wife, who operated a retail greenhouse business, contacted me to ask if I would ever be interested in working for a nursery in Wellsboro, approximately thirty-five miles away. It was a wholesale business with twelve greenhouses. She had been in touch with them and found out that they were looking to hire more help, at least temporarily. She wondered if I would be interested and if I felt that physically I would be able to do the work. I had had a homeowner size greenhouse for years and growing plants and flower gardening had been a major hobby for me. I agreed that I wanted to give it a try. She went with me the first day and worked alongside me. Finally, by the end of the day one of the two owners came to me and asked if I was interested in working there every day. I immediately responded with a resounding yes. He noted that I was using a cane and questioned if I could do the physical labor. I told him that I was willing to try if he would let me.

The next day I started and worked there for three growing seasons. They began growing in the fall and everything was sold out by the end of May. It was perfect for me. It supplied us with some additional income and, best of all, made me feel useful again. The best part was that it was work that I truly enjoyed. I already knew more about the plants and growing needs than many other people they had in the past. They gave me the opportunity to be a foreman of sorts and organize the work of the other workers. It was an opportunity to utilize skills I already had.

The pay was only minimum wage at first, but that wasn't the most important thing to me at that time. The point was that I was doing something useful and I enjoyed it, not to mention that I was out of Peggy's way for a few months each year.

Journal Entry
April 21, 2003

It is once again past a date when my attorney had expected an important decision from the US attorney's office. Every time the mail goes or the phone rings I expect a message from him. There was some encouraging news a couple of months ago as two other cases similar to mine were dismissed. My attorney has told me that our judge is under no obligation to do the same and that there are some small differences between my case and those dismissed. We pray fervently for dismissal.

Each day as I move one step closer to knowing the outcome of my case I feel like a person walking slowly out on a frozen lake. I don't know if the ice will hold and I will be safe or if it will break and I will be plunged into the icy depths.

Journal Entry
June 2, 2003

1. I'm struggling to get my "fight" back and yet I am trusting the Lord, placing all my faith in Him.
2. Loneliness seems to overwhelm me sometimes. Even though I am surrounded by friends and family who love and support me, I feel alone. It is a loneliness I have felt for most of my life. It is that loneliness that goes with knowing some-

thing bad about yourself that no one else knows—only now of course everyone does know.

3. It is hard to plan. I don't know if I will be here one month from now, three months from now or a year from now. Will I be here for Christmas this year or next year? How would all of this be explained to my grandsons?
4. My job at Tioga Nursery is coming to an end for the season. Should I be looking for another job? I have loved working with the plants, and the people are wonderful. Thank you Lord for providing work that keeps me busy and that I truly enjoy!
5. I have been having much trouble sleeping again. When I get up in the night I am exhausted the next day. I've had strange dreams where I wake up startled because in the dream I am about to be hurt or killed in one of various ways, often by drowning. Example: I am on a train that derails and goes under water.

Physical Problems Worsen

Through the three seasons that I worked at the nursery my issues with falling and dizziness and tremors continued. I was getting physical therapy, vestibular therapy, and getting placed on a stretching machine to try to release pressure from compressed nerves in my lower back. I was seeing various neurologists, each with a little different twist on what the problem might actually be.

In the spring of 2003 I had forty-one consecutive days of migraine-like headache accompanied by all my normal ongoing physical symptoms. I knew that some people thought they were all psychosomatic, probably caused by the stress. The only thing is, I started all of them prior to the legal problems and some of them had been part of my history since I was a teenager.

I continued to battle depression, fatigue and a variety of other symptoms. The fatigue was overwhelming many times and all I wanted to do was sleep.

The falling was by far the worst symptom to deal with. I never knew when it would happen until I was in the process of going down. My legs often felt like they weighed a ton and I scuffed along as I walked. I fell in the house, in the driveway, the garden, in my greenhouse and in the greenhouses at the nursery where I worked.

Chapter 12

LIVING WITH UNCERTAINTY

Fall 2003 and all of 2004

The next several months all begin to run together for me now. There was a continuation of many of the same problems and blessings, and the health issues never ceased to add a little more drama to my life.

We were blessed by the fact that some friends kept in close contact with us and invited us to their homes or came to visit us. However, many friends made no contact at all. I tried to not let it bother me, but I did wonder if they just didn't know what to say or if they were truly repulsed by what they perceived that I had done. Occasionally, we would meet some of them while out shopping and they always seemed very friendly. Some apologized for not contacting me and confirmed that they just didn't know what to say. I noted to myself that I would try to never be like that with my friends. Simple communications were so important to me, even if it was just saying, "I'm thinking of you or praying for you."

One of our former pastors and his wife, Dick and Barbara Boothe, maintained continual contact over the years. The pastor's wife and Peggy became best of friends and corresponded for years after they moved to Lynchburg, Virginia. Barb was one of the first people with whom Peggy shared my legal situation, not only because she was a good friend, but also she had become a counselor after moving to Lynchburg. I wanted Peggy to have someone like that to talk to since I believed she needed someone to confide in who would be a good listener and friend.

Four of the Pathways Board members kept in touch and invited us to their homes for dinner occasionally or invited us to attend a community event with them. Two other former Board members kept in touch through email messages regularly. These contacts were very important to me. It helped to alleviate some of my feelings of loneliness and worthlessness.

I continued to attend regular counseling sessions with Dr. Bryant in Williamsport and was required to make a monthly contact with the Federal Probation Department person in Williamsport also. Again, I was not officially on probation at that time, but while we waited to find out about the disposition of my case, I was required to be supervised by a person from the Probation Department.

Counseling Progresses

Dr. Bryant was a tremendous support in guiding us through the long waiting periods and constant uncertainty. He helped me to understand that, although we were uncertain about the final course of action that the court would take, we could be very certain that God would never forsake us. He continually reminded me to remember "who I am in Christ" and to keep this event from defining me for the rest of my life. That was difficult to do since it seemed in many ways that life was at a standstill until some resolution could be determined.

I still struggled with depression and then guilt from being depressed. I thought that if I was truly trusting the Lord I should be able to wait without getting depressed. The long waiting and anticipating the possible outcome, as well as the lack of being able to continue my career were all impacting me emotionally. I thought back about the professional life I had enjoyed and the reputation that God had allowed me to have in my chosen field. I became angry at myself when I reflected on the fact that my own destructive actions had destroyed it all and caused a major setback in my testimony for Christ. Depression was the natural follow-up to that scenario.

Dr. Bryant provided the perfect sounding board and was the encourager for both Peggy and me. There were many weeks that we could hardly wait for our time with him. He constantly said that he could not imagine what it would feel like to be in our positions. He believed that it was all so unfair from the legal standpoint. Since he knew the most private pieces of my life and what had transpired, it was a comfort just to hear him say those words.

Physical Problems Diversify

The physical problems never came to a complete close, but there were some improvements, even as some new symptoms developed. The medication changes that my doctor had implemented, at the recommendation of the specialists I had seen, were helping to at least alleviate the severity of the migraines, although I still had them several days per month. Fatigue continued to be a major complication in my life.

I still continued to have problems with weakness in my legs and some falling. However, I was beginning to get severe pain in my lower back. I had experienced this type of pain to a certain degree for years, but it was getting more severe and now I was taking pain medication to deal with it. Again, I was receiving physical therapy to try to address that problem.

Spoke at a Pastors' Meeting

On January 12, 2004 I spoke at a meeting of pastors in Duryea, Pennsylvania. It was held at the church where our son, Patrick, was an Assistant Pastor. The group, consisting of approximately eighteen to twenty men, met monthly. Usually one of them preached a message and they discussed various pertinent topics. Patrick asked me to come and share my story as far as it was completed at the time and be available to answer questions. I misunderstood the timeframe and filled the whole meeting time. I didn't realize that they had planned to have one of the pastors preach as well. They decided to forgo that for the month, but I was embarrassed when I found out that I had talked too much.

It was the first time that I had stood before a group of strangers and admitted my abuse and my failure in getting trapped with the Internet sin/repent cycle. Even though I knew that this was a group of pastors, I also knew that Internet pornography was a tremendous problem for people from all walks of life and any age group. My intent was to share how God had intervened in my life to rescue me and I wanted to encourage anyone who might be in a similar situation to seek help immediately.

Also, I wanted to alert these pastors to the fact that I had been a deacon and Sunday school teacher when this problem developed in my life. It was very likely, given the statistics regarding the percentage of people who are either addicted or at least deliberately dabbling with visiting pornographic websites, that they had people in their own congregations who were struggling with this problem.

I shared with them a statistic I had recently read that over forty percent of pastors admitted on an anonymous survey that they visited pornographic websites at least once per month. Of course, I had no idea about any of the pastors present there that day, but I was pleased with the number of questions they asked and the further information they requested individually as they came up to me afterwards.

Christian Ministry Opportunities Continue

Christian Counseling: In spite of the widespread local knowledge about my legal situation, I continued to get calls from people to counsel them for various issues in their lives. I did this for no charge as a ministry outreach from our local church. I always checked to see whether they were aware of my legal status before agreeing to meet with them. I never met with anyone who was not aware of it. They usually told me that their knowledge of it was what made them more comfortable with me because they knew I would not likely be condescending toward them regarding their issues.

It was reassuring to me to have the opportunity to meet with people in that manner. As a result of my ongoing issue there was no way I could be condescending. It was a blessing that the Lord allowed me to function in that important area. In some ways it seemed as though He was showing me that I would eventually be able to be restored as He promised in 2 Peter 5, and that my experiences would be useful in helping others. I could now speak with a new burst of confidence about God's faithfulness and His power to help us overcome even the greatest and most grotesque of problems.

Teaching and Preaching: On May 9, 2004, I was asked to substitute for our pastor and preach the sermon that day. At first I didn't believe I should do it, but our pastor and church Board members encouraged me. They reminded me that I had stood before the congregation two years earlier, confessed my error, asked for their forgiveness and told them that I knew that God had already forgiven me. They also knew that I was still pursuing counseling and were acquainted with me personally very well. I finally agreed and experienced great joy and relief for doing it.

Additionally, I was asked to return to teaching the adult Sunday school class on a rotating basis along with other men from the church. This, too, got me into studying the Word even more and helped to renew my confidence. These events led me to believe that somehow God was going to restore me once again to a place of service after the whole legal affair was finally resolved.

Bible Study with Friend from Church: Throughout the whole legal affair I continued to meet weekly with a friend from church to do Bible study. He and I had been meeting since before the FBI search in November of 2001, and we never stopped after the arraignment and public humiliation in July of 2002. He and his wife told us that the day my story made the local news in 2002 they came immediately to our door. Since we were camping with our sons and their families, we missed their visit, but so appreciated their concern. In all, he and I participated in Bible studies together for approximately five years.

Other Church Involvement: Peggy and I continued to sing special music at church occasionally and I was often asked to lead congregational singing. At times I was asked to conduct prayer meeting on Wednesday evening when the pastor had to be away.

In some ways it was like old times, except I knew that it wasn't. I often wondered if there were people in the congregation who resented my involvement in any type of leadership role. However, I had informed the pastor and deacons that my attorney had told me he had seen cases linger on for years without any resolution. He believed that my case could be like that since the Assistant Federal Prosecutor had already indicated that he was in no hurry to move it forward. The pastor and deacons informed me that they were satisfied with my spiritual life and they saw no reason to keep me in the background any longer. I still refused to get involved with any programs at church that involved the children.

Home Depot Interview

On June 24, 2004, I was fortunate to get an interview at Home Depot. I was pleased because I had applied for other positions and was never called for an interview. I met with two men and had what I thought was a good interview until the very end. The job application asked if I had ever been convicted of a felony or if there were any legal charges pending. Of course, I had to answer yes, just as I had on all the other applications. The men asked me if I would be willing to share the circumstances around this legal issue. I was pleased to be able to get a chance to describe what had happened and hoped that they would not see it as a reason to reject me.

As I was explaining what my legal situation was they began to look rather skeptical. They leaned back in their chairs, closed the file folders they had in their hands and stated that they could not believe a person could be prosecuted for simply viewing free material on the Internet. I told them that I hadn't met anyone in the past three years who could believe it, including a couple of attorneys I knew.

They then wished me luck and the interview was over. I never heard another word from them.

My attorney informed me that unless a job application asked about legal questions, I was under no obligation to bring it up myself. In fact, he advised me to not mention it. He also cautioned me to avoid applying for any position that involved working with children. I already knew that was out of the question.

Back to the Greenhouse Work in the Fall of 2004

In October of 2004, I once again returned to work in the greenhouses in Wellsboro. It was again a joy and gave me a boost as far as my mindset and attitude were concerned. I still had frequent headaches and occasionally fell, but I wasn't using the cane at work at all. By this time I was feeling very confident in the job and even initiated a new way of keeping track of incoming orders to make sure we were growing the right plants in the proper timeframes to be ready for shipment when the customers wanted them.

Although I truly enjoyed this work, it did take its toll on my body. I had lots of aches and pains and the problems in my back seemed to be increasing. I never complained to the owners because I didn't want them to worry about me and I wanted to be able to do all that everyone else was asked to do.

Employment at a Garden Center

By spring of 2005, one of the owners of the greenhouses told me about the possibility of an opening as a manager at a local garden center. The starting date for the position was near the end of the greenhouse season so it would not take me away until we were nearly finished for the year. I submitted an application and was interviewed by the owner soon after. He offered the job as manager and I transitioned into it over a period of about ten days by working a few hours at each place.

Once again, I was amazed at how God had worked it out so that I could work at a job that I loved. A person who had been there for years was a tremendous help to me. She did not want to be the manager, although she had done the work of the manager for years.

I had been a manager in the human service field for many years, but this was a whole new ballgame. I had to learn what was expected of me, mostly from my coworker. I put in significantly more hours than I was paid for because I so badly wanted to do a good job. I came in early and stayed late to try to keep up with all that was to be done. In the early part of the summer, the garden center was open on Sunday afternoons, which meant that I could go to church at 10 o'clock, but needed to leave immediately to open the center at noon.

There was constant pressure to make the garden center operate as efficiently as possible in staffing. I learned that there was no desire by the owner to increase the availability of garden center merchandise such as gifts. The biggest and most important items to be sold were trees shrubs.

In all of my jobs over the years I had never had any problem relating to other people in management or to my supervisor. In this case, I had very little communication with the owner except when he told me about something that displeased him. I told him that I would do anything in any fashion he wanted, but that I wished that he would tell me what he wanted done. He told me, "I would think that a person with your experience and educational background would know what to do." I wanted desperately to make it through the summer season, but wasn't sure that I would last. I believed that there was definitely something wrong here, but could not figure out what it was at that point.

Peggy's Intercessory Prayers

During the summer of 2005, Peggy developed a list of comforting scriptures she had come across in her devotional time, or that were given to her by friends, that seemed to relate to the struggles we were experiencing. In our counseling Dr. Bryant had suggested how powerful it is to actually pray the words of scripture back to God. These scriptures were examples of God's promises and assurances to us.

Peggy not only read these scriptures every day, she actually began to pray the words of these passages. I believe that those verses were an important part in getting us through this ordeal and certainly did influence the final outcome. I heartily recommend this practice to anyone going through a serious struggle.

I believe so strongly in the power of praying God's Word that I have included the verses that Peggy found and employed in our situation in Appendix A. I am sure there are hundreds more, but those were the ones that helped us.

Chapter 13

MOVEMENT ON THE LEGAL FRONT

The Proposal: Within two or three weeks of starting the job at the garden center, my attorney called to tell me that he had been informed by the Federal Prosecutor's office that they were ready to get my case off the books. He indicated they were proposing that, in return for discontinuing my challenge to the legality of the charge against me, they would agree to recommend to the judge that I get only probation and a fine with no incarceration. I was shocked because I had come to believe that it was going to go on for years, and Peggy and I had been praying for total dismissal for the past three and a half years.

I told him that I needed to talk it over with Peggy because we would never make a decision like that without praying about it first. He cautioned me to not wait too long because the Federal Prosecutor might decide to withdraw the offer and proceed with sentencing as was planned in 2002.

The Decision: After three and a half years we were at another important crossroad. We had prayed all that time that the charge would be dropped, and yet it now appeared that the prosecution would go forward, but in a somewhat different manner than originally threatened. Peggy insisted that she had been praying fervently all of the verses noted earlier and that she could not believe that God was going to ignore all of that. I agreed with her, but reminded her that now they were promising no incarceration even though my attorney and the Harrisburg attorney had been adamant that there would definitely be some period of imprisonment. It seemed to me that God was intervening in a big way, plus, I wanted this state of indecision in our lives to be over so we could move on to whatever God had planned for us.

We prayed together and separately about the offer. My attorney, Mr. Tice, was not sure how much the fine would be and whether I would be required to register under Megan's law. While those were major issues to me, they were not worth risking the possibility of being incarcerated. Peggy came to the point where she told me that I would have to make this decision since I was the one who would have to live with the consequences. Mr. Tice reminded me that several of the challenges from other people who had been discovered in the FBI sting were still unresolved. He wanted me to know that if I accepted this offer and later the courts threw out the cases of the other defendants, I could not recant my guilty plea, but that my sentence would be carried out. He also informed me that from all he had been able to discern, it was unlikely that those defendants were going to win their challenges.

After a couple days of praying and consulting with some wise Christian friends, I decided to accept the offer from the Federal Prosecutor. When I notified my attorney, he informed me that he and the Assistant Federal Prosecutor would now set up a meeting with the judge to present this proposal. He told me that this type of arrangement was highly unusual for the charge that had been leveled against me, but since the proposal came from the Federal Prosecutor's office and both were in agreement, the chances were excellent that the judge would agree also. He told me to be prepared, however, that the judge might seek some other resolution that included some shorter period of incarceration or in-home detention or perhaps even electronic monitoring. While I was not looking forward to any of those alternatives, they still were better than the original thirty-six to forty-eight months of incarceration that I was told I would likely receive.

I asked Mr. Tice if I could be present for the meeting with the judge, but he didn't think either the judge or the Assistant Federal Prosecutor would agree to that, and even he did not recommend it. He thought everyone present would feel hampered by my presence. Therefore, people I barely knew, and who knew very little about me, were going to meet behind closed doors to make a decision that would affect the rest of my life and that of my family.

The Meeting: I felt uneasy on the day that the meeting finally occurred a few weeks later. Peggy and I had our two oldest grandsons with us that week, so we took some time to do some special activities with them that day. My attorney had told me that he would call me in the evening to let me know the outcome. Around 8 o'clock he did call and we talked for approximately an hour. He said that the judge did ultimately agree to what they were recommending, but it was not an easy process. The judge told them that the U.S. Attorney General was watching closely how Federal judges were ruling on various types of cases and child pornography was one of the top ones. Mr. Tice reported that after much discussion, and the unusual situation where the Assistant Federal Prosecutor was agreeing with him in an attempt to convince the judge, he was still uncertain that the judge was going to be in agreement.

Finally, the judge asked the attorneys to leave the room and he consulted with his court staff. When they were invited back into the judge's chamber, the judge agreed to go along with their joint recommendation of no incarceration, but probation and a fine would likely still be part of the sentence. He did not offer any other alternatives. Mr. Tice said that that was not the time for him to ask how much the fine would be and whether I would be required to register under Megan's law. He also told me that he would now negotiate to have the three years I had spent under court supervision through the probation department counted toward whatever term of probation the judge decided to give me. However, he was not optimistic about that happening and reminded me that I should be very satisfied with this resolution to my case.

Mr. Tice told me that I would be getting letters from the Federal court regarding a new sentencing date and from the Federal Probation office regarding updating all the data that we had delivered to them in July of 2002 prior to the arraignment. A new presentencing report would need to be completed and sent to the judge for his consideration.

Letters of Support: Mr. Tice asked me to get letters of support from anyone who I thought might write convincing statements to give the judge a better sense that he was making the right decision as agreed upon. Some people had written letters three years earlier when we thought sentencing was going to be in 2002. I now had the opportunity to ask even more people. Peggy took a very active role by contacting people personally or sending out email letters asking friends, neighbors and former professional associates to consider writing a letter of support. Letters were to be sent directly to Mr. Tice who would deliver them to the judge at the appropriate time. In all, thirty letters were sent to Mr. Tice. After the sentencing was over I was sent copies of the letters. I was overwhelmed with gratitude by the comments from people. I am so thankful to everyone who took the time to write. It was clear that these were not letters jotted off in a few minutes, but rather painstakingly written from the hearts of the people.

A Petition to the Judge: One of the professional people, who I had been associated with in Corning as part of my duties as Executive Director of Pathways, asked if it would help to get a petition in support of me signed and sent to the court. I asked my attorney about it and he again agreed, but wanted to be the one who wrote the paragraph at the top of it. A few days later I received his copies of the petition and Peggy began taking them around the community, among family and professional associates. Even family members helped to get signatures. Some of my former professional associates took copies and circulated them among their associates. Over the course of two weeks, two hundred fifty-five signatures were secured from people from all walks of life. I was amazed at some of the names I saw on that petition. People who I had not heard from over the three and half year waiting period had signed it. It taught me to not be judgmental just because someone had not reached out to me.

The petition was circulated among people in our own church and in a neighboring church where the pastor had actually asked for prayer for me during the Sunday service.

He also passed the petition around during the adult Sunday school class in his church..

I appreciate Peggy's diligence and that of so many who took the petitions around. It was not an easy thing to do. I also appreciate all who signed the petition knowing it was going to a Federal judge. There was concern by some about what impact their signing might have on them in the future

Sentencing Date Set

Receiving the letter from the Middle District of the Federal Court informing me that my sentencing date was August 29, 2005 was a devastating event for both Peggy and me. It was a little like watching a loved one slowly die. You know it's going to happen, but it is still a shock when the day finally arrives. We knew the sentencing was coming soon and we even knew the major portion of what the sentence was supposed to be, but that didn't change our anxiety about it.

Concern Regarding News Coverage: One of the things that Peggy and I had prayed about since the day of the FBI search on November 19, 2001 was that the Lord would see fit to spare me from devastating humiliation in the news media. Of course, it would also be humiliating for Peggy as well. The Lord chose a different path for us in the days and weeks after my arraignment in July of 2002, when He allowed at least five articles to be printed in local newspapers, including two headlines, and also television and radio coverage. As I noted earlier, much of the information was misleading at best, since I was only guilty of visiting the websites that had the child pornography and never possessed any form of hard copies, as did the other people discovered in the sting. That information never seemed to make it into the news coverage, although there was one statement by a person from the Federal Prosecutor's office indicating that my case did not appear to be as serious as the others, but there was no further explanation given.

We prayed fervently that this time after the sentencing the Lord would spare us from horrible and embarrassing news coverage. My heart ached for Peggy and other members of our families. It hurt so badly when I realized how much pain I had brought upon these loving and supportive people.

Informing the Garden Center Owner: Once I received the date of the sentencing, I knew I needed to meet with the garden center owner to inform him about my whole legal situation. I met with him early one morning before any other staff arrived. When I was finished, he informed me that he already knew about my situation, not in the detail that I had explained though. He told me that one of his customers, who also knew me, had reported it to him. He said he was very disappointed that I had not been "man enough" to tell him. I apologized and thanked him for allowing me to stay. We agreed that I would only work until the end of that week and then take a leave of absence until we saw how the news media covered the sentencing. Neither of us wanted his business to get mentioned in the reporting. That arrangement also gave me the opportunity to inform the other staff who I had been working with every day. I now knew why I had felt a strain in the relationship between the owner and myself. After the sentencing, I never went back to inquire about future employment at the garden center.

Sentencing Day Arrives

On the morning of sentencing I was more upbeat than one would think I should have been. I don't think it was because I was pleased with what I thought the sentence would be, but because the nearly four years of waiting and feeling as though life was at a standstill was about to be over.

My attitude was that I wanted the sentence to be pronounced, served, and thus end this ordeal we had been living through.

Several members of my family joined Peggy and me in the Wegmans' parking lot across from the Federal courthouse shortly after eight AM. Both of our two sons were there along with seven other members of our family. Additionally, a long time-friend who was member of my Board at Pathways surprised me by joining the family as well.

Since we were early, we all went into Wegmans and enjoyed coffee and each other's company for a few minutes. One person told me that I seemed very relaxed for someone who was going through this experience. I was relaxed and felt confident that the Lord was going to bring us through this ordeal stronger and more mature as Christians. My trust in Him could not have been stronger. Soon we left and walked across the street where we met Mr. Tice. We all had to be checked through the metal detector and then proceeded up the elevators to the courtroom.

Back to the Beginning

We are now back to the point at which I started this story in chapter one. The Assistant Federal Prosecutor finally arrived and the court was called into session. All the legal preliminaries were completed and the charge against me was once again read. The judge asked me if I had anything I wanted to say before the sentence was pronounced. My attorney had told me that if I spoke to keep it to five to seven minutes because the judge would get frustrated if it went longer. However, in the whole entire three and a half years that preceded that day I had not been allowed to say anything except "guilty" at my arraignment. I had not been allowed to write a rebuttal to the misinformation in the local newspapers or talk to the media at all. Therefore, I wanted to take advantage of this opportunity to say what the Lord had laid on my heart. I knew it wouldn't change anything concerning what the judge had decided regarding the sentence, but at least some people would hear about it and it would be part of the public record.

My Statement in the Courtroom: The most important thing to me was that I give God the glory for bringing us through this situation and express my continued faith that He was going to use this experience in my life to help others in some way. I again apologized and thanked my family and our church family for all of their love, prayers and support since this ordeal started. I was able to share Philippians 1:12

which says, *"But I would have you to understand, brethren, that the things that happened unto me have fallen out rather to the furtherance of the gospel..."* I pointed out that, even though this whole legal affair was a terrible thing, it had given me an opportunity to grow in my faith and to share it with others. I said that if it was God's will, I was willing to speak and write and do all that I could to help others keep from getting snared in the trap I was in. I told the judge that Psalm 37:24 says that, "*though he fall, he shall not be utterly cast down: for the Lord upholdeth him with His hand.*" I reported that I had fallen, but I surely was not utterly cast down. The Lord had picked me up and I was ready to hear the sentence and then get on with my life to serve God any way He desires.

The judge never took his eyes off me as I spoke and I never looked away from him. He appeared to be truly listening. When I was finished nearly twenty minutes had passed and the judge stated that my comments were among some of the most eloquent and heartfelt he had ever heard in his courtroom. He thanked me and asked the Assistant Federal Prosecutor if he had anything further to say. His only comment was that he agreed with the judge's statement and that he was encouraged to hear what I had to say.

Sentence Pronounced: The judge asked my attorney and me to approach the front rail below him. He then read a prepared set of sentences as follows:

1. Three years of Federal Probation
2. Six thousand dollar fine
3. Ten years of registration under Megan's Law
4. Ongoing counseling during the period of probation

I was shocked and greatly saddened at the requirement to register as a sex offender. My attorney told me to not get too excited because he would see about appealing that part of the sentence. I was pleased that the fine was only $6000 since it could have gone as high as $250,000. I was told to report to the Probation Office downstairs to set up an appointment.

Immediate Reaction

After I met briefly with a person in the Probation Department, I joined my friend and family outside. At that point I was feeling great relief that it was over. Again, as I look back I was probably inappropriate in how joyful I seemed. I encouraged everyone to join Peggy and me at the Perkins restaurant that was within walking distance from our vehicles. I thanked them all for coming and we enjoyed a brunch together. I was laughing and talking a lot and felt like a child at his birthday party.

Afterwards, I hugged everyone and thanked them again for being there to support me. They left and Peggy and I departed to get groceries and do some other shopping. As the day wore on my lofty jubilation came crashing in on me. I sat in the car while Peggy was in one of the stores and I began to feel the reality and magnitude of the events of the day. I no longer had to wait to see what the Lord was going to do with the legal situation. It was upon me now. I was officially a convicted felon, a criminal in the eyes of the law, and a sex offender at that.

My temporary and false jubilation melted into a heavy dark feeling. When I shared that feeling with Peggy she said, "I wondered how long it was going to take. Everyone knew you were just putting up a front for them." In reality, I wasn't consciously putting up a front. I truly was relieved and joyful that the court scene was over. That was all I could see at that point. Now I had to face the reality of three years of trips to Williamsport each month to meet with the probation officer and ten years of registering with the State Police as a sex offender. The humiliation continued. Now we would wait to see if the news media would once again destroy me over the next few days.

Peggy's Email Update to Our Friends

We both thought that it was important to give a report to all those who had been praying and writing letters for us on the results of the sentencing. Once again, Peggy took the lead and composed the following letter and sent it out to approximately 40 people.

Dear Friends and Family, August 29, 2005

Tonight we find ourselves very confused because, although the day did not go as badly as it could have gone, it did not go well. The sentencing went just as our attorney had predicted-the felony stands, there is a $6000 fine and three years of probation. However, we were really set back when the judge required Bruce to "register" in the state in which he resides, at level one. Furthermore, there were two reporters in the courtroom. We had prayed fervently for weeks that the Lord would prevent that from happening as well as asking the Lord that if it could be His will, that He would remove some of the other penalties. I had prayed continually for five specific requests and none were granted. On a spiritual level I understand that God has a plan that I cannot yet understand, but on a human level I am still struggling with the "why." People have been praying from Arizona to Texas, Brazil, Florida to Canada and everywhere in between. I had had such a calm and peace during the last week that the Lord was going to do something really special before or during this sentencing, but I guess it was not meant to be. Immediately after the sentencing was over our attorney stated that he plans to appeal the sex offender registration requirement because he does not feel that it is applicable in this situation, so please make that your next matter of prayer on our behalf. The attorney had thought that this was not going to even be an issue today.

The best part of the whole day was that Bruce was able to speak for 15-20 minutes! The judge was extremely attentive and visibly moved during that time. When Bruce was done the judge said that "Those were the most eloquent, sincere and heartfelt comments I have ever heard in a criminal case and I will long remember them." Then the judge asked the Assistant US attorney for any comments. He responded by saying that when he had entered the courtroom he came in with 5 reasons why Bruce should be granted probation, but now he was adding a sixth reason-apparently he was also favorably impressed. Unfortunately, it didn't make any difference in their decision. The judge also acknowledged that he had read the thirty-two letters of support and the petition and that he was impressed with them. Thank you to all of you who helped Bruce in that way. It really was beneficial.

During Bruce's time to speak he was able to share the following verses of scripture, Psalm 37:23-25 "The steps of a good man are ordered by the Lord and He delighteth in his way. Though he fall he shall not be utterly cast down, for the Lord upholdeth him with His hand. I have been young and now I am old, yet I have not seen the righteous forsaken nor his seed begging for bread." He closed by saying that he realized that the only failures in life are those who refuse to get up and go on and that he is ready to "get up and go on."

Our next BIG obstacle is going to be the media coverage in the next few days! We can see it now – they will major on the sex offender status, not knowing that our attorney is appealing it, nor should they know at this point I would guess. We are very concerned especially for Pathways and what the fallout may mean there. It seems like so many of the things that we have envisioned, had nightmares/dreams about etc. etc. over the last nearly four years, eventually come to pass.

Bruce stated a couple of weeks ago that throughout his life he had “won a lot of battles” but in the end he was going to “lose the war.” He was referring to the fact that his abusers had told him that he was “worthless and always would be worthless” and that when everyone sees the news, so many will believe it. But we are also quick to say that they can never take away the most important things in life – our faith and our salvation! We are so thankful for that.

We met with the counselor this afternoon to debrief. That was very helpful and we are returning again next week. We are so thankful for such a Godly compassionate counselor.

Tomorrow, Bruce has to call back to Probation and schedule an appointment to discuss what happens from here on, to set up a payment plan for the fine, give a DNA sample and who knows what else.

Once again, we just want to say thank you to all of you for your prayers and encouragement to us. I think we are going to need lots more over the next several weeks, but we know the Lord is with us and will give us strength and peace and we are so thankful for that.

Always,

Bruce and Peggy

Chapter 14

ADJUSTMENT AND RECOVERY AFTER SENTENCING

Morning Aftershock

The morning after sentencing Peggy and I sat in the living room and stared at the floor and out the windows. Her sister and brother-in-law's family was having an open house that day to display their new dairy barns and milking parlor. The facilities were directly across the road and up the hill from our house. Unaware of whether the local paper had articles about me, I had already vowed that I was not going to show my face that day.

Peggy looked so sad and confused. She said, "I was so sure that God was going to rescue you from that prosecution and sentencing. I prayed so hard and long for it and nothing we prayed for turned out the way we had hoped." I said, "Well, do you think God was unable to save me from the prosecution." She replied, "Of course I know He was able to, I just don't understand why He didn't." I replied that, "We both know that God could have spared me from it all, but for some reason He chose not to." I explained that the only way I could view it was that it was His will to let me go through this. I had prayed for the last three and a half years that if it was His will He would let this situation pass without any incarceration, but that I would accept whatever His will might be because I knew that He would not allow anything to happen that was not for my good and His glory. Since He had allowed it then we had to trust that He had some specific reason and plan for it all. As Joseph explained to his brothers in Genesis 50:20 *"…you thought evil against me, but God meant it unto good."* I knew that Peggy believed this as well, but the morning aftershock was a little numbing.

This attitude is what has brought me through all the years since November of 2001 when the FBI came to search our house. I had prayed to be rescued from the trap I knew I was in, and this is the way God chose to bring it about. I just needed to be humbled before Him and follow His leading in my life so that I wouldn't miss the plan He had for me. I placed a copy of Jeremiah 29:11 on my computer printer. It reads, "*For I know the thoughts that I think toward you, saith the Lord, thoughts of peace, and not of evil, to give you an expected end.*"

Another verse that provided great peace of mind was Jeremiah 17:7-8, *"Blessed is the man that trusteth in the Lord, and whose hope the Lord is. For he shall be as a tree planted by the waters, and that spreadeth out her roots by the river, and shall not see when heat cometh,but her leaf shall be green; and shall not be careful in the year of drought, neither shall cease from yielding fruit."* There is great reward to those who trust in the Lord, and I vowed never to lose my hope and trust in Him. I knew that Peggy would be right beside me with those same thoughts. She is the most trusting and faithful Christian I have ever known.

God Provides Blessings Again: As Peggy and I sat in our living room discussing the topics noted above, my brother, Carl, and his wife Ellen came driving in to greet us. They brought two turkeys and the morning papers. There was nothing in the local newspapers and a decent article in the Williamsport paper. That article said "Local man pays big price for sneaking a peak at child porn." I was thankful that it was not on the front page. It also reported on my statements to the judge and quoted the judge's comments after I spoke. I thought it was as fair as it could be.

Soon, Peggy's sister, Carol, and her husband Cecil came to the door and they also brought a meal for the day. What a blessing it was for us. The Lord had already turned our hearts to joy as His blessings kept coming. Next, Ross Perry and his wife Mary Lou came to our house with food as well. Ross had been in the courtroom with us the day before. All three couples were there at the same time and we appreciated them so much. Could there be any doubt that God had orchestrated this rescue as well? We had been in a melancholy mood as we sat by ourselves in the living room and now our home was filled with laughter and happiness.

Three Years of Probation

A few days after sentencing I was back in Williamsport to meet with my probation officer and to get blood drawn for a DNA test. He was always very accommodating to make my appointments on the same day that I had an appointment with my counselor so that we had to make only one trip. During one of my appointments at the Probation Department, one of the officers looked over my file and said, "Boy, you must have connections with the man upstairs. I've never known anyone with this charge against them who didn't serve time somewhere." Peggy and I both thought this was our opportunity to give God the glory for intervening and guiding us through this ordeal. One of us told him, "We do have connections because people all over the country and even in some foreign countries have been praying about this for the last three years." He responded by saying, "Well, I guess it worked."

Over the course of the three years I had three different probation officers. I was always treated fairly and politely. For the most part, they never made me feel like a criminal. There were, however, some requirements by the Probation Office that complicated out lives tremendously.

First, I was not allowed to travel out of state without prior written permission. That requirement was particularly difficult because we live in Pennsylvania, approximately a quarter mile from the New York State border and all of our medical appointments and shopping were usually done in New York State. I would no longer be able to go with Peggy for shopping or any form of entertainment, such as visiting friends, without prior approval. I did get approval for doctor appointments because even though my doctors were in Sayre, Pennsylvania, we had to travel through a section of New York to get there. All of my physical therapy appointments were also in New York State, so approval for those was required as well.

Eventually, we started doing all our grocery shopping in Williamsport once a month. Peggy came to enjoy the stores in that area because they were in close proximity to each other and we didn't have to do much driving around. We usually bought lunch from the McDonalds' Dollar menu and that was a treat too. Occasionally, when we were marking some special date or significant milestone in our journey, we would treat ourselves and go to Olive Garden or some other restaurant.

Another part of the travel restrictions that was bothersome was that I could only travel in the Pennsylvania counties that were included in the Federal Justice Department's Middle District. There were several counties in that district and our oldest son's county was included; however, our younger son lived in a county just over the Middle District line, so we had to get prior written approval to visit him. I was never denied a travel permit, but it took some planning and time to get the approval coordinated each time.

Second, at my first official appointment with the probation officer I was informed that a monthly report had to be filed with him. It required information about residence, employment status, a list of all vehicles and their VIN numbers and mileages. I also had to report whether I had been in contact with any other felon during the past month and whether I or anyone in my household had been questioned by a police officer that month. One time Peggy was stopped by the State Police for having a headlight out on her car and we had to report that. She was pretty upset to think that now her name was in the official records of my case.

Also included on the monthly report were the balances of all accounts such as checking, savings, retirement, etc. We also had to list any payments we had made in the previous month that were over $500, what they were for and an indication of the account from which the funds had been taken.

Some of the time when I went in to meet with one of the officers Peggy was allowed to join me. I always felt more comfortable with that arrangement because I wanted her to hear anything they had to say. Occasionally, in my private sessions with an officer, I was asked about my viewing of the images on the Internet. In particular he wanted to know if that was still a problem for me. Fortunately, I was able to report that we didn't have Internet in our house and that those issues had already been dealt with in my counseling sessions.

We made monthly payments on the $6000 fine and sent a check with each monthly report. When we came to the end of the first year we were told that we now had to again complete the massive amount of documentation that we had already done two other times for them as part of the presentencing work. After questioning my probation officer about why we would have to do that again, he informed us that as long as we still owed money on the fine we would have to do this report annually. It took several days for Peggy to pull out records and complete the report each of the previous two times, all because of my mistakes. We immediately decided that we would pay off the fine. We had to withdraw money from my retirement account to do it, but it was worth it to avoid having to complete this lengthy report each year.

Registration under Pennsylvania Megan's Law

My attorney sent me a letter a few days after sentencing to tell me he had discussed his idea of appealing the requirement for me to register as a sex offender. He said that the judge would not agree to that since he believed he had already gone above and beyond his normal course of action by waiving any incarceration time. While I did not like that response, I could see how the judge was coming to that conclusion. I was so thankful for the leniency he had already shown. My attorney indicated that we could still appeal, get denied, and then appeal to an Appeals Court, but that would likely bring into question the lesser penalty that my judge had given. It could result in losing the current sentence and having a new one imposed with much greater restrictions. We decided to drop the idea of appealing and I had to go to the State Police to register.

I have to go in September every year for ten years. It is another humiliating experience. First, I have to walk up to a window and tell the person what I am there to do. Sometimes there are other people waiting in the lobby who hear me say those words. I realize that neither they, nor the police officers doing the registration, understand why I was ordered to register. I always assume that they mistakenly believe that I have physically abused some child.

I still struggle sometimes with understanding why I have to register, since I only viewed images, by myself, on a free website in the privacy of my home. However, I have been told that the important point is that if no one visited those websites there would be no motivation for the real criminals to create the images and place them on the Internet. Those people most definitely were abusing the underage children when they photographed them. For anyone to view them online makes him part of the vicious cycle.

The first time I registered I was required to indicate residence, place of employment, educational facility attending, if any, all vehicles with descriptions and VIN numbers. I was fingerprinted again and had to have two or three mug shots taken. Each time there is any change in any of the information reported on the records I have ten days to go back and have the records changed and get the mug shots taken again.

At the time of this writing I have completed five of the ten years required. During that time I have had to return to the State Police barracks three separate times apart from my regular annual requirement. I had to return once for employment change and two times because of a change in the vehicles I own. The vehicle registration requirement includes all recreational vehicles such as a camper, boat, boat trailer and any vehicle that is garaged at my residence even though it may not be registered in my name. Needless to say, I try to not make many changes; however, due to the fact that we have to drive older vehicles, we have had to make changes on two occasions.

The other ramifications of being listed on the sex offender list are not as severe for me as they might be for someone else. We have no intention of living anywhere other than in the home we built over thirty-nine years ago. Therefore, I don't have to be concerned about a neighborhood protesting my presence. Our neighbors all know about my situation and are good friends and very supportive. In order to prevent any accusations, I never put myself in any situation where I am alone with anyone under eighteen years of age. I am around children, but either Peggy, the parents or other adults are always present.

Internet Restored

After much prayerful consideration, Peggy and I decided to get the Internet reinstalled on our computer within a few weeks after my probation period ended. We had learned to live without it over the past six and a half years, but there were many times when we wished it was available to us again. I had explored the newest blocking software and Internet security so that we would have precautions that had not been there at the outset of my problems a few years earlier. We were able to block pop-ups, install an excellent virus blocking system along with Internet accountability software.

The accountability software we chose is called *Covenant Eyes.*[4] It has Internet blocking capability, but also monitors every website accessed on my computer and sends a weekly report to Peggy and our pastor as my chosen accountability partners. When you know that all the websites you visit are going to be reported within a week to someone else, the *Covenant Eyes* software is a powerful resource and a major disincentive to explore potentially dangerous areas on the Internet. Our local church set up the account and there are several individuals who have taken advantage of it.

Employment

My brother-in-law, Walter Barnes, and his two sons, Jim and Jeff, operate their large family farm next door to our home. After the sentencing and subsequent loss of my job at the garden center, he asked me if I would be interested in working part-time for them. My job would entail feeding calves and young cattle at 6 AM and 3:30 PM seven days per week. I was thrilled with the offer. I am still not sure if the offer was because they really needed me or if it was an act of kindness to help us out. That would be characteristic of him. The job was a perfect fit for me. I could walk to work, wear old clothes, and had the freedom to request days off to visit our sons or to go for doctor appointments. I did the farm work for nearly three years until my physical problems became too great a hindrance for me to continue.

By the time my ten years of registration as a sex offender are finished I will be sixty-nine years of age and hopefully will not have to be applying for jobs at that point. In 2008, both Peggy and I started receiving Social Security and that has been a life saver financially.

Financial Distress

The farm work paid slightly above minimum wage and that was a great help. However, we still had to withdraw a significant amount each month from our retirement account in order to make ends meet. That was unfortunate because it impacted our future income. Our financial advisor where our retirement account is invested kept warning us to be careful about spending.

We were very careful about spending. Peggy shopped very seriously and always took advantage of specials and sales. I am sure that we ate less flamboyantly than most people. We had a large garden and Peggy diligently canned and froze food every year. We learned to have mostly meat-less meals. We bought an extra freezer so that we could increase our storage. The fact that we did the major amount of our grocery shopping only once a month was also a saving for us. Peggy always stocked up on sale items and developed quite a pantry. Furthermore, we almost never bought name brands of anything.

One side impact of our financial stress was that we learned to enjoy shopping at dollar stores and thrift stores. Peggy shopped all year for little gifts for the grandchildren at the dollar store. The thrift stores became a fun place for both of us to shop. We occasionally found brand new items for a fraction of their original cost. One of Peggy's biggest joys was going to the clearance rack and finding slacks, blouses or sweaters that fit her and looked great for only a dollar each. I don't think anything made her any happier than knowing she had found a bargain. I think she appreciated it more than if she went out and paid $100 for a dress. I sometimes found new high-quality shoes for only $4.

It is an amazing example of God's grace and watchful care over us, when I think of how he provided for us during these years of low income. Numerous people sent or gave us money and many times just at the times we needed it most. I recall one time when our hot water heater quit working. We wondered how we would find the money to pay for a new one. That very day we received a check in the mail from a friend for nearly enough to buy the new water heater. We had other instances where that same person surprised us with a check in the mail just at a time we needed it most.

Another precious example of how God's people care for one another occurred at Christmas. We received a check from a young family who we barely knew. The young gentleman's parents attend the same church as us and they had been told about our plight. It seems that all year this couple placed all their spare change in a jar and then at Christmas they determined how they could use it to bless someone else. We had the privilege of being blessed by them on one of the first Christmases after the legal issues began.

Another time when we were attending a special service at a neighboring church a man came up to me, handed me an envelope and asked that I not open it until I got home. When I did there was $200 inside. Again, praise God for his matchless love and grace towards us.

Natural Gas Leasing and Royalties: A totally unexpected blessing from the Lord has been the entrance of several natural gas drilling companies into our area. We had been fortunate enough to purchase approximately ninety-two acres of land a few years before the legal issues began. The property included a house which we rented out and that income nearly covered the mortgage and the taxes. Once we started to experience serious financial difficulties we considered selling the property and using whatever profit we derived to help with daily living expenses. However, we saw that as a last resort because it had excellent hunting woods, and our sons enjoyed coming home to hunt there. That was one of the main reasons we purchased it.

Fortunately, we did not reach the point of last resort because we were again blessed when we were approached by one of the gas drilling companies who wanted to lease our mineral rights. Then, when they drilled in the future we would receive royalties on the gas they pumped from under our land. In a very short time all of that did come to pass.

We received lease money and then the drilling took place on the property next to ours so we started receiving royalty payments. We have not received a great amount yet, but the promise and prospects are there. Also, it is a blessing that the land that includes our acreage was among the first to be drilled in our local area. God is never late and never early, but always right on time with His blessings.

Pastoral Encouragement

In February of 2006 the Lord brought Mr. Harold Burrell to become the new pastor of our local church. He and I began having long discussions on the phone and face to face soon after his arrival. I wanted him to know everything about my legal situation and my lifetime struggle. He was unbelievably supportive. He also encouraged me to write about it and prepare to go out to speak if the Lord should lead in that direction. He and his family spent years on the road as a musical evangelistic team and he has hundreds of contacts. He offered to help me get started when I was ready.

Soon we began meeting on a weekly basis for prayer. We prayed for each other and for people in our congregation and community at large. Now we have opened that to any men who wish to join for prayer on Saturday mornings.

Pastor Burrell continues to be a constant source of support and encouragement to me and I value his counsel on spiritual matters.

Major Unexpected Blessing

In the late winter of 2008, Peggy and I received a phone call from my friend Matt Orkins, who I have mentioned in a couple of other chapters. After some small talk he asked, "Do you guys have passports?" I replied that we did not and never had needed them. He said, "Well, go out tomorrow and start the process of getting them because you are going on an all-expense-paid cruise." In shock I asked, "What are you talking about?" He explained that he and his wife, Linda, wanted to take us on a cruise to celebrate the conclusion of my probation restrictions at the end of August. I said, "We appreciate your unbelievable intentions, but there is no way we could accept such an offer. That is just out of the question."

Without going into all the rest of our discussions about the offer, on September 28, 2008, we were flown to Miami, cruised the western Caribbean for seven days and flown back home, all at no expense to us. God again provided in a way that we would never have expected or imagined. We are so grateful to God and to Matt and Linda for their unspeakable kindness to us.

The Three years in a Nutshell

All in all, the three years of probation did seem to go by rather quickly. What we had thought would be an inconvenience going to Williamsport on a monthly basis ended up being something we looked forward to doing. We turned it into an enjoyable outing, something that we never did on a regular basis prior to the legal issues.

Peggy and I grew closer together and closer to the Lord than we had ever been. I was home nearly all the time and we traveled together, read the scriptures together and prayed together. We experienced God's hand of mercy and grace first hand.

We continued to go to counseling on a monthly basis as was required by a condition of my probation. Our insurance wasn't paying for it so that was an additional expense; however, we gladly paid for it because it was so very helpful to us. The turmoil and shock to our whole being that came as a result of the prosecution was truly life-changing. Dr. Bryant skillfully guided us through the rough waters and always kept us focused on Christ

Chapter 15

SPIRITUAL VICTORY: RELEASE FROM THE SNARE

I attribute my healing to God and Him alone. But, I credit my personal interactions with two people and the writings of a third for greatly influencing me and pointing me to the healing powers of God's Word as I made my journey to freedom from the snare.

Dr. Timothy Bryant: The first is Dr. Timothy Bryant, from Cornerstone Family Health in Williamsport, Pennsylvania. I was referred to him by a local Christian counselor who was a friend of ours. That friend became like the Good Samaritan who picked us up from the side of the road when we were desperately hurting. He administered the immediate spiritual first aid that we needed and by God's grace and wisdom referred us on to Dr. Bryant who became like the innkeeper in the Samaritan account, caring for us for the long run. Peggy and I met with him for over 100 sessions over a six year period. The first six months we voluntarily went to him, but after my arraignment in July of 2002 the judge ordered me to be in counseling and we were blessed that I was allowed to stay with Dr. Bryant.

The first task for Dr. Bryant was to try to support both of us who were devastated by the arrival of the FBI to search our house and the realization that most likely life was going to change drastically very soon. The fact that I had to finally come forth with the truth about my past to Peggy and others was like opening an old wound for me, and it created a new wound for her as she feared the legal ramifications. For both of us, concern and fears about our future were almost paralyzing.

And then, there was the shame of it all. I was ashamed before Peggy, our attorney, our friend, the local counselor, and mostly before God, even though I knew that He knew about it all along. Equal to assisting me to handle my shame was the fact that I had to deal with my past abuse and the lifelong impact on me. I was glad that I was finally going to attack that issue directly, except I had hoped it would be under different circumstances. Perhaps the Lord knew that if I hadn't done so during all those years I wouldn't do it unless I was forced in some way.

Dealing with the Abusive Experiences: I mentioned elsewhere in this book a small portion of the process Dr. Bryant used to help me deal effectively with the abusive experiences and the way they impacted me. I had to think back and revisit those situations and view myself as the "little boy Bruce," remembering how I felt then and every aspect of those events that I could remember. I then had to consider how I thought God would have viewed me at those times. I had to consider, "Did God see me as a bad and shameful person then?" and, "Was what others did to me truly my fault, no matter what my abusers said to me?"

I needed to reflect about my abusers and consider the question, "Was I angry at them?" I always had said I was not angry because I voluntarily participated in those despicable actions. However, one of my homework assignments was to think back in detail about those events and write down on paper their actions toward me. I did that and I shared it with Peggy. As I did, floods of anger came spewing out of me.

I was angry and always had been angry, but was afraid to show it or felt unjustified to show it. After all, in my way of thinking it was my fault. Now I could see that it was not my fault and that God had already forgiven me the first time I had asked Him years ago. I needed to accept the truth of His promises and realize that *1 John 1:9 "If we confess our sins, he is faithful and just to forgive us our sins, and to cleanse us from all unrighteousness,"* applies to me.

Dr. Bryant said he wasn't sure there was anything for me to confess in the first place, but if I felt convicted about what had happened, then asking for God's forgiveness should end the matter. My problem was that since I didn't believe I deserved forgiveness, I could not accept the fact that God had actually forgiven me.

Then, I was presented with a question that changed my way of thinking about this whole forgiveness issue. If God said I was forgiven, and I didn't believe He did forgive me, am I calling God a liar? That thought brought me to tears. It was a major turning point in all of my counseling. Knowing that God was for me, had accepted me and saw me as clean and fit for His kingdom changed everything for me. I would no longer have to strive to be perfect and just achieve, achieve, and achieve in order to be worthwhile in God's eyes.

Letting the Light Shine on my Woundedness: One of the next areas I needed to consider was opening the secret places in my life that were causing me pain and letting the light shine upon them. That meant talking about all the areas of woundedness that I felt and not keeping them secret any longer. Only as I talked about them and applied God's Word to them could I feel the sense of relief and freedom that I was seeking. As I did, it was like releasing the pressure that had built up for years. I was no longer carrying around secret burdens that dragged me down mentally, emotionally and spiritually. In fact, I wanted to talk about my newfound freedom so much that Peggy had to caution me to not overdo it with other people. She told me that people probably got tired of hearing me talk about it.

Remembering who I am in Christ: I had lived nearly my whole life struggling with the feeling of worthlessness. Now, though I had been able to see that God did not see me as worthless because of my participation in the childhood abusive situations, I still battled that feeling because of the legal battle I was going through and all the public humiliation involved. One of Dr. Bryant's continuing themes that he mentioned at almost every counseling session was, "Remember who you are in Christ!" In chapter 8 I listed the many verses he pointed out to show that God sees me as anything but worthless. That should have ended the discussion unless, of course, I chose not to believe God, and I was not going to go down that road again.

An additional thought that Dr. Bryant emphasized with me was the truth that "I cannot let my current circumstances define me for the rest of my life." That, too, was a struggle for me to accept at first. But I came to the realization that what appears, for the moment, to be a devastating and hopeless situation, can be used by God to change my course in a new direction and area of service that would not otherwise have been feasible. If I only viewed my circumstances in comparison to the professional life I had been accustomed to living, then I was devastated. But, if I viewed my situation as possibly God opening the door for new opportunities of service, I could see hope and a future. My whole mindset became one whereby I only wanted what God wanted for me. I trusted Him explicitly because I thoroughly believed that He would only allow what was good for me and what would bring glory to Him. That was all I could ask or hope for through the entire ordeal.

Living out of Christ: One of the most important concepts that Dr. Bryant shared with me was what he called "Living out of Christ." It is based on the principles taught in John chapter 15 regarding the vine and the branches. The branches get life from the vine and as Christians we get life by living out of Christ. Here are the concepts embodied in Dr. Bryant's *Living out of Christ* [5] paper which were so helpful to me. I have underlined and added the personal pronouns in order to adapt it to fit my needs.

In order to live out of Christ:

1] I must realize and embrace <u>my position in Christ.</u>

   a. God sees me as acceptable to Himself as Christ is to Himself, because I have the righteousness of Christ as a free gift. 2 Corinthians 5:21

   b. Christ abides in me. He abides in me and I in Him. John 15: 1-11

   c. My position in Christ is His gift to me.

d. This gift is for His glory and is a great privilege for me.

2] I must <u>distinguish between the truth and the lies</u> Satan would have me believe.

a. I am cherished and belong to God.
b. Realize that truth is to be embraced above what feels true. Christ died for me and loves me no matter what I may have done or how unworthy I feel.
c. My lack of understanding of a biblical truth does not negate it.

3] I must understand that Living out of Christ is a <u>lifestyle to be boldly lived</u> daily.

a. Christianity is at the core, a relationship initiated and empowered by God in which He arranges to come and rule within me.
b. I need to renounce daily [or more frequently] my rights to manage myself and acknowledge my dependence on Him.
c. Admission of my powerlessness and living humbly is key to living out of Christ.

d. I am enhanced and completed by Christ coming and dwelling in me.

4] I must recognize that my old nature has been crucified with Christ.

a. This belief releases me from the bondage of my past.
b. There is a war going on between my flesh and my new nature. I need to allow Christ to rule and free me from worldly habits.

5] I must realize that people cannot satisfy my need for significance.

a. Only God can make me feel any worth or value.
b. True joy, peace, safety and security come only from Him.
c. No amount of effort on my part will produce these results.

6] I must believe that my being holy is about Christ being Holy in me, not me trying to duplicate goodness on my own.

7] I must understand that the fruit of the spirit are just that, fruit or attributes of God in me, not my developed character.

8] I must demonstrate through my behavior that God desires me to live through Him, not just for Him.

a. He wants me totally yielded to Him.
b. He wants to love and serve people through me, rather than for me to mimic His behavior on my own.

In summary, the above principles mean I must always remember who I am in Christ because He loves me and has given me His righteousness. That is a settled matter. Satan tries to get me to believe his lies about myself every day; even after I have turned my back on him for days, months or years he tries again and again to convince me that I am no good. I will not believe that lie from Satan because to believe Satan is to disbelieve God. I need to allow God to manage my life daily because whenever I try it will always end in failure. I am powerless without Christ. I am released from the bondage of my sinful past because my old nature has been crucified with Christ. People are important, but they cannot make me feel significant because it is only God who can make me feel any worth or value. I will fail if I try to duplicate Christ's goodness on my own. I must allow Christ to be Holy through me. He wants to demonstrate the fruits of His spirit through me. God wants me to live through Him, not just for Him; and therefore I must be totally yielded to Him all the time.

Erwin W. Lutzer: Erwin Lutzer does not know me, but I would like to meet him someday. He has written many books, but the one that has been a source of inspiration and healing for me is the one titled, *After You've BLOWN IT: Reconnecting with God and Others.*[6] It is a small book of only 87 pages. Perhaps that is why I have read all of it three times and parts of it many times more than that. I felt relief the first time I read it because he points out that no matter what our sin may be or how badly we have messed up, God wants to reconnect with us and will forgive us if we yield unto Him and trust Him.

Lutzer makes the point that there is no one that is so undeserving of redemption that God will not forgive him and re-establish fellowship with him. I fell into the trap of at least partially believing Satan's lies that God could not truly love me because I was unworthy. He points out that in the account in scripture of the prodigal son, the son returns home after working at feeding pigs for a living, but says to his father, "*I have sinned against heaven, and in thy sight, and am no more worthy to be called your son.*" *Luke 15:21b.* Even after the son had wasted his inheritance on riotous living, his father loved him and rejoiced over his return. Of course, this is a picture of our heavenly Father accepting us when we turn from our sin and come running home to Him.

Lutzer points out that it is difficult for some of us to accept God's grace. We recognize that we have sinned and hate our sinful past. Sometimes we end up hating ourselves as well. We think our sin is too great for our heavenly Father's forgiveness.[7] But in the account of the prodigal, the father kissed his son, welcomed him home and put a clean robe on him. This was a sign of total forgiveness shown by a loving father. I realize now that my heavenly Father was waiting for me all those years that I lived in shame and regret.

He further reflects on the fact that we need to separate out conviction feelings from guilt feelings. The Holy Spirit convicts us so that we will repent and ask for forgiveness. That conviction makes us feel guilty until we are able to ask God for forgiveness. Satan, however, continuously tries to convict us over and over again to make us feel guilty for sins for which we have already been forgiven. That cycle makes us miserable and we feel unworthy again.

Lutzer touched on a tender spot with me when he pointed out that some people try to get rid of their guilt by doing good deeds. A long time ago I had claimed Matthew 5:16 as my life verse. It says "*Let your light so shine before men, that they may see your good works, and glorify your Father which is in heaven*". If someone tries to do that I'm sure that many good things will come from it. However, if the reason he is trying to do good works is to relieve his own guilt over sinful or perceived sinful behavior, then his motives are wrong and it is unlikely that the Father in heaven will be glorified by them. I am afraid that many times I have been guilty of trying to overcome guilt by doing good works. What I actually needed was to believe that when God says I am forgiven, it is true, and that settles it.

Finally, Lutzer refers to the person who says he believes that God has forgiven him, but states that he cannot forgive himself. How ridiculous of us to assume an attitude like that. What does that say about us and our arrogance to act as though we are holier than God? If He forgives, then how can we not forgive also? I had to come to the realization that

God had forgiven me and truly believe it, then let go of the feelings of worthlessness and accept God's grace.

Cyndy Sherwood: The third person I would like to credit with having influenced my spiritual healing is Cyndy Sherwood, from His Healing Light Ministries, Colorado Springs, Colorado. I have only recently had the pleasure of meeting Cyndy and have become familiar with her tremendous work in the development of a healing curriculum she titles *The Healing Journey.*[8] This curriculum is a 29 week class which takes a participant from their place of pain and despair, metaphorically referred to as Egypt in her material, through many tedious steps, including mountains and valleys, on the way to freedom from their woundedness, which she calls the Promised Land. Cyndy has also written a book which is a narrative version of the whole 29 week curriculum that she has titled *Roadmap to Healing: Following the Biblical Path to Freedom, Peace and Joy.*[9] Within the book she has included a novella, which is the account of a wounded healer who has already traveled the arduous road from Egypt to the Promised Land. She is now going back to Egypt to guide another wounded soul through the trails she must travel to break free from the grip of her past and the victim mentality, into the place of freedom, peace and joy.

I had the privilege of being taught by Cyndy for four days, read her excellent book and I am now co-leading two classes of men through *The Healing Journey*[10] curriculum. Her material has been like the glue that holds together all that I have learned and come to understand previously about my own woundedness and healing process. It is like putting the proverbial "icing on the cake". If I had not had any counseling or read any other material, I would have found peace and healing in Cyndy's work, although I am delighted that I had the privilege of experiencing both.

In her curriculum, *The Healing Journey*[11], Cyndy takes us back to the Genesis account of the Israelites being led out of Egypt toward the Promised Land. In that account, we see that the Lord allowed them to wander in the wilderness for forty years. They needed that time to discover their identity and to see that they were totally dependent on God. Oh, how I can relate to that experience. I did not have to wander for forty years, thankfully, but I had to wait nearly four years before I knew my destiny and another three years living through God's choice of consequences for my actions. Those were my wilderness years of life. I, too, needed to be reminded continuously of who I was in Christ, in other words, to understand my identity.

One of the big issues that arose for the Israelites was that they were starving and murmuring to Moses that they would rather be back in Egypt. God again provided for them by sending down manna from heaven six days per week. They were to take only just enough for the one day and then pick up more the next day, except for Friday, when they would pick up enough for two days so that they would not have to gather on Saturday, the Sabbath. If they gathered more than they needed for the one day, it would stink and be filled with worms or maggots by the next morning. In this manner, the Lord was teaching them to trust Him for their provisions and not try to provide for themselves.

Three critical concepts that are paramount in Cyndy's material are her emphasis on three principles about God. 1] He is my provider, 2] He is my protector, and 3] He is my source of power. Any time that I chose to put myself in the place of God regarding any of those principles I was doomed to failure and pain.

I did put myself in those positions, sad to say, many times. I worked diligently throughout my life to try to prove my worth. I thought I had to achieve, and achieve some more, to be seen as worthwhile, even if only by myself. It never worked. My striving on my own always had maggots without fail. There was never any lasting satisfaction from anything that I achieved on my own. I needed to recognize that God was my provider and lean upon Him to give me the peace and joy that I longed for throughout life.

Part of my striving to achieve was also my way of trying to protect myself from those who told me that I was worthless. My providing and protecting issues worked very closely together and I often put myself in the place that God should have been in my life. I always knew that God was there, but I viewed Him as just looking over my shoulders to see if I would do the right thing and then scowling if I did not. I thought He expected me to solve my problems on my own. I have learned that He has all the answers and He wants to give them to me if I am willing to yield myself to Him and seek Him daily.

The third principle that Cyndy stresses is that God is our source of power. As I look back now, I realize that I wasted a lot of energy and created tremendous stress for myself because I did not take advantage of the power that God wanted to give me. Only He could resolve the issues that I struggled with in life. I tried many different avenues to relieve my pain and nothing ever lasted or else did not work at all.

As I noted in an earlier chapter, I sought Dr. Bryant's help in finding out what had caused me to think that visiting the horrible website would, in any way, help to resolve my issues. His response fits clearly into the three principles Cyndy talks about here. He said that I may have been trying to heal myself or provide therapy to myself. Unfortunately, I chose a very unhealthy and unsuccessful manner in which to do it. I see now that I was neglecting the power available through God and not taking advantage of His role as my provider and protector. Now, as I have the privilege of working with other men, and listen to them tell their life stories, it is easy to understand that they, too, have put themselves in God's place at certain critical points in their lives and are now reaping the troubles that naturally follow.

Both Cyndy Sherwood and Dr. Bryant emphasized the significance of the false beliefs we allow to influence our thinking. I certainly did that. I believed the lies that Satan planted in my mind about myself, and the natural consequence was that I did not believe the truth about God. I could never bring myself to admit that I was angry with God. That would have been an entirely unacceptable concept to me.

However, since I had the false belief that God had not protected me as a child, I slipped into the mode of ambivalence toward Him because that was easier than acknowledging that I was angry with Him. I don't think I was conscious of the fact that it was really anger that I was harboring over the years. Once I realized that truth about God's character and how he actually views me, I was finally able to have peace.

Much of the work that Cyndy has put together coincides with what I learned through my counseling with Dr. Bryant. I had to learn to let go of the past, stop viewing myself as a victim, and realize that I am forgiven as a new creature in Christ. I had to learn to forgive others and stop letting my anger eat away at me like an acid, even if the other party didn't think they had done anything wrong.

These three individuals and their work have been major sources of help in getting me on the road to healing and becoming a helper of others myself. I hasten to add, lest anyone get the wrong impression, that I recognize that all three of these individuals noted above, and many more like them, are only instruments in God's hands. It is God and His Holy Spirit that does the healing. What a joy it is to know that God loves me and wants, more than anything, to help me and give me peace and contentment. I am so glad that I have found that peace and don't have to live in sadness and darkness anymore. I no longer have to wear that mask that makes me appear to be someone I know I am not. That is true freedom.

As I made my journey through trying and difficult times, I finally realized that I had been caught in a snare that Satan had tailor-made for me. I was trapped by my own self-centered desires and drives. He convinced me that God may have saved me as I asked Him to, but he would certainly never embrace me and love me because of the filth of my sin. Rather, He would hold me at arm's length, like the poor step child in the story of Cinderella, who was never really accepted into the family. I realize now that was just another lie from Satan that I had believed when I was caught in his snare. It became evident that it was actually I who was holding God at arm's length.

I hope it was evident as you read about my lifelong struggles that Satan was continuously pulling at me. Sometimes his trap was more like a weight around my ankles holding me back. If I did succeed at something, I thought it was by my overcoming the resistance of that weight, which required great personal effort. I often did not recognize that it was

God who empowered me or that He could have made the situation more bearable if I had just relied on Him more.

Through most of my life I was unaware of the truth of Psalm 124:7. This verse states that we are already escaped from the snare. The problem is that many of us act as though we don't know that Christ has already set us free, so we struggle on alone instead of taking advantage of the power that our loving, merciful, heavenly Father wants to provide for us.

Praise God for His promises. Satan is truly like the fowler who snares birds, only we are the poor birds he seeks to catch. God's word says in *Psalm 91:3 "Surely, He shall deliver thee from the snare of the fowler, and from the noisome pestilence"*. God wants to deliver each of you just as he has delivered me. He has already paid the price for our souls. He has already broken the snares that hold us. All we have to do is recognize His work on the cross and step free.

"The snare is broken and we are escaped." **Psalm 124:7**

Critical Steps in My Recovery Process

The following steps are those that I discovered were essential in my adjustment and successful recovery. I share them here in the hope that they will be of help to someone else.

I had to:

1. **Confess, repent and ask for forgiveness and cleansing.**

   "If we confess our sins, He is faithful and just to forgive us our sins, and cleanse us from all unrighteousness." 1 John 1:9

2. **Humble myself totally before the Lord.**

   "Humble yourselves therefore under the mighty hand of God, that He may exalt you in due time: Casting all your care upon Him; for He careth for you." 1 Peter 5:6-7

3. **Pray, multiple times per day.**

"Evening, morning and noon, will I pray, and cry aloud: and He shall hear my voice." Psalms 55:17

4. **Find a prayer and accountability partner, someone who knew about my struggles and who would be available to me at any time.**

"Brethren if a man be overtaken in a fault, ye which are spiritual, restore such an one in the spirit of meekness; considering thyself, lest thou also be tempted." Galatians 6:1

"Bear ye one another's burdens and so fulfil the law of Christ." Galatians 6:2

5. **Seek Godly counseling.**

"Blessed is the man that walketh not in the counsel of the ungodly, nor standeth in the way of sinners, nor sitteth in the seat of the scornful." Psalms 1:1

6. **Read God's word and renew my mind.**

"Thy word is a lamp unto my feet, and a light unto my path." Psalms 119:105

"And be not conformed to this world: but be ye transformed by the renewing of your mind, that ye may prove what is that good, and acceptable, and perfect, will of God." Romans 12:2

7. **Resist the devil. Rid myself of access to things that may make me fail.**

"Submit yourselves therefore to God. Resist the devil and he will flee from you." James 4:7

8. **Change the things I think about.**

"Finally, brethren, whatsoever things are true, whatsoever things are honest, whatsoever things are just, whatsoever things are pure, whatsoever things are lovely, whatsoever things are of good report; if there be any virtue, and if there be any praise, think on these things." Philippians 4:8

9. **Limit time spent alone.**

"For where two or three are gathered together in my name, there am I in the midst of them." Matthew 18:20

10. **Associate with Godly friends who knew about my struggle, who would encourage me.**

"And let us consider one another to provoke unto love and good works. Not forsaking the assembling of ourselves together, as the manner of some is; but exhorting one another: and so much the more, as ye see the day approaching." Hebrews 10:24-25

Chapter 16

YOUR SNARE HAS BEEN BROKEN TOO

Do you feel as though you are caught in some sort of trap or snare in your life too? It doesn't matter what it is, because remember, Satan tailors his snares to fit each of our individual lives. He knows where our weak spots are and he will zero in on them as much as possible.

Perhaps you have been caught up in adultery, gambling, alcohol, drugs, stealing, vulgar language, dirty jokes, swearing, lying, lust, pornography, covetousness, gluttony, apathy toward God, failure to read His Word, pray or attend church regularly, or even workaholism. All these, and likely many more, are snares or traps that Satan uses to draw us away from the peace, joy and abundant life that God intends us to have.

Some of you may believe there is no hope for you or that your sin is too big or too bad for God to forgive. There is no such thing. That thought is a lie from Satan and he has been very successful with it for centuries. But, now you know the truth. No matter what you are ensnared in, God has already broken that snare for you. All you have to do is believe in his finished work on the cross, accept His free gift of salvation and forgiveness, and start seeking His will for you every day.

I visualize concepts to help me get a better grasp of them. When I think about Psalm 124:7, which states *"The snare is broken and we are escaped,"* I see a picture of a net with the mesh torn apart and birds flying freely out of its grasp. The birds are white doves symbolizing purity.

Each of us can be like those white doves. God has already provided the way for us to escape from our snares. I urge you to not let another day go by in bondage to your sinful habits, godless lifestyle, or being ensnared by believing Satan's lies about yourself. Turn to God right now and yield yourself to Him. Determine to turn your life over to Him and seek Him diligently. He has a blessing for you and He wants you to live in peace and contentment starting today.

You might pray a prayer something like the one below:

Heavenly Father, I come to you right now with a heavy heart.

I know that Satan has me trapped in ________________ ________________.

I want to be free from his grip and I know that you have already provided the way of escape for me.

I claim that promise right now and ask you to forgive me.

By the power of your Holy Spirit give me the strength to "fly" free from this snare.

Help me to resist Satan's attempts to prevent me from following you.

Help me to find Godly counsel and support to grow in my walk with you.

In Jesus name I pray.

Amen

If you have never asked Jesus to become your personal savior, that is the first task you must do. After you have done that, He will provide His Holy Spirit to become your comforter and guide. You might pray a salvation prayer similar to the one below.

Heavenly Father, I come to you now confessing that I am a sinner and I cannot save myself from the punishment that I deserve.

I believe that You sent Your son Jesus into the world to shed His blood on the cross to pay the penalty for my sin.

I pray that you will forgive me now for my sins and I accept Jesus as my personal savior.

Thank you for saving me from the hell that I had deserved.

Help me to live for you daily.

In Jesus name I pray.

Amen

Appendix A

The Bible verses that Peggy prayed.

"Now unto Him that is able to do exceeding abundantly above all that we ask or think, according to the power that worketh in us." Ephesians 3:20

"But the God of all grace, who hath called us unto eternal glory by Christ Jesus, after that ye have suffered a while, make you perfect, stablish, strengthen, settle you." 1 Peter 5:10

"For in the time of trouble He shall hide me in His pavilion: in the secret of His tabernacle shall He hide me; He shall set me up upon a rock." Psalms 27:5

"The Lord will give strength unto His people; the Lord will bless His people with peace." Psalms 29:11

"My times are in thy hand: deliver me from the hand of mine enemies, and from them that persecute me." Psalms 31:15

"Thou art my hiding place; thou shalt preserve me from trouble; thou shalt compass me about with songs of deliverance. Selah." Psalms 32:7

"Our soul waiteth for the Lord: He is our help and our shield. For our heart shall rejoice in Him, because we have trusted in His holy name. Let thy mercy O Lord, be upon us, according as we hope in thee." Psalms 33:20-23

"The righteous cry, and the Lord heareth, and delivereth them out of all their troubles. The Lord is nigh unto them that are of a broken heart; and saveth such as be of of a contrite." Psalms 34:17-18

"Delight thyself also in the Lord; and He shall give thee the desires of thine heart." Psalms 37:4

"And the Lord shall help them, and deliver them: He shall deliver them from the wicked, and save them, because they trust in Him." Psalms 37:40

"…I wait patiently for the Lord; and He inclined unto me, and heard my cry. He brought me up also out of an horrible pit, out of the miry clay, and set my feet upon a rock, and established my goings. And He hath put a new song in my mouth, even praise unto our God: many shall see it and fear, and shall trust in the Lord." Psalms 40:1-3

"Be pleased, O Lord, to deliver me: O Lord, make haste to help me." Psalms 40:13

"…God is our refuge and strength, a very present help in trouble." Psalms 46:1

"As for me, I will call upon God; and the Lord shall save me. Evening, and morning, and noon, will I pray, and cry aloud: and He shall hear my voice. He hath delivered my soul in peace from the battle that was against me; for there were many with me." Psalms 55:16-18

"Cast thy burden upon the Lord, and He shall sustain thee: He shall never suffer the righteous to be moved." Psalms 55:22

"What time I am afraid, I will trust in thee. In God I will praise His word, in God I have put my trust; I will not fear what flesh can to me." Psalms 56:3-4

"...Be merciful unto me, O God, be merciful unto me: for my soul trusteth in thee: yea, in the shadow of thy wings will I make my refuge, until these calamities be overpast." Psalms 57:1

"...Deliver me from mine enemies, o my God: defend me from them that rise up against me." Psalms 59:1

"...Truly my soul waiteth upon God: from Him cometh my salvation. He only is my rock and salvation; He is my defence; I shall not be greatly moved. How long will you imagine mischief against a man? Ye shall be slain all of you: as a bowing wall shall ye be, and as a tottering fence. They only consult to cast Him down from His excellency: they delight in lies: they bless with their mouth, but they curse inwardly. Selah." Psalms 62:1-4

"...Hear my voice, O God, in my prayer: preserve my life from fear of the enemy." Psalms 64:1

"Deliver me out of the mire, and let me not sink: let me be delivered from them that hate me, and out of the deep waters. Let not the waterflood overflow me, neither let the deep swallow me up, and let not the pit shut her mouth upon me. Hear me, O Lord; for thy lovingkindness is good: turn unto me according to the multitude of thy tender mercies. And hide not thy facve from thy servant; for I am in trouble: hear me speedily. Draw nigh unto my soul, and redeem it: deliver me because of mine enemies." Psalm 69:14-18

"...Make haste, O God, to deliver me; make haste to help me, O Lord. Let them be ashamed and confounded that seek after my soul: let them be turned backward, and put to confusion, that desire my hurt." Psalms 70:1-2

"But I am poor and needy: make haste unto me, O God: thou art my help and my deliverer; O Lord, make no tarrying." Psalms 70:5

"O God, be not far from me: O my God, make haste for my help. Let them be confounded and consumed that are adversaries to my soul; let them be covered with reproach and dishonor that seek my hurt. But I will hope continually, and will yet praise thee more and more. My mouth shall show forth thy righteousness and thy salvation all the day; for I know not the numbers thereof." Psalms 71:12-15

"...Thou which hast shewed me great and sore troubles, shalt quicken me again, and shalt bring me up again from the depths of the earth. Thou shalt increase my greatness, and comfort me on every side." Psalms 71:20-21

"My tongue shall talk of thy righteousness all the day long: for they are confounded, for they are brought unto shame, that seek my hurt." Psalms 71:24

"Be merciful unto me, O Lord: for I cry unto thee daily." Psalms 86: 3

"Give ear, O Lord, unto my prayer; and attend to the voice of my supplications. In the day of my trouble I will call upon thee: for thou wilt answer me." Psalms 86:6-7

"He that dwelleth in the secret place of the most high shall abide under the shadow of the Almighty. I will say of the Lord, He is my refuge and my fortress: my God; in Him will I trust. **Surely He shall deliver thee from the snare of the fowler,** [my emphasis] and from the noisome pestilence. He shall cover thee with His feathers, and under His wings shalt thou trust: His truth shall be thy shield and buckler." Psalms 94: 1-4

"He shall call upon me, and I will answer Him: I will be with Him in trouble; I will deliver him, and honor him." Psalms 91:15

"I called upon the Lord in distress: the Lord answered me, and set me in a large place. The Lord is on my side; I will not fear: what can man do unto me?" Psalms 118:5-6

"The Lord shall preserve thee from all evil: He shall preserve thy soul." Psalms 121:7

"But mine eyes are unto thee, O God the Lord: in thee is my trust; leave not my soul destitute." Psalms 141:8

"Attend unto my cry; for I am brought very low: deliver me from my persecutors; for they are stronger than I. Bring my soul out of prison, that I may praise thy name: the righteous shall compass me about; for thou shalt deal bountifully with me." Psalms 142:6-7

"The Lord is nigh unto all them that call upon him, to all that call upon him in truth. He will fulfil the desire of them that fear Him: He also will hear their cry, and will save them. The Lord preserveth all that love Him: but all the wicked will He destroy." Psalms 145:18-20

"For I know the thoughts I think toward you, saith the Lord, thoughts of peace, and not of evil, to give you an expected end. Then shall ye call upon me, and ye shall go and pray unto me, and I will hearken unto you. And ye shall seek me, and find me, when ye shall search for me with all your heart. And I will be fond of you, saith the Lord: and I will turn away your captivity, and I will gather you from all the nations, and from and the places I have driven you, saith the Lord; and

I will bring you again into the place whence I caused you to be carried you away captive." Jeremiah 29:11-14

"Fear thou not; for I am with thee: be not dismayed; for I am thy God: I will strengthen thee; yea, I will uphold thee with the right hand of my righteousness." Isaiah 41:10

"The king's heart is in the hand of the Lord, as the rivers of water: He turneth it whithersoever He will." Proverbs 21:1

"They compassed me about like bees; they are quenched as the fire of thorns: for in the name of the Lord I will destroy them." Psalms 118:12

"I know that the Lord will maintain the cause of the afflicted, and the right of the poor. Surely the righteous shall give thanks unto thy name: the upright shall dwell in thy presence." Psalms 140:12-13

"And this is the confidence that we have in Him, that, if we ask anything according to His will, He heareth us: And if we know that He hear us, whatsoever we ask, we know that we have the petitions that we desired of Him." 1 John 5:14-15

Endnotes

1. Schwartz, Bernard and Paul Wood, *How to Get Your Children to do What You Want Them to do,* Prentice Hall, 1977.
2. Bryant, Timothy, "Who I Am in Christ." A list of scripture references presented as part of counseling sessions. Cornerstone Family Health, Williamsport, PA, 2002.
3. Chambers, Oswald, *My Utmost for His Highest*, Oswald Chambers Publication Association, Ltd. 1963. Quoted in *Our Daily Bread,* RBC Ministries, Grand Rapids, MI, January1, 2002.
4. Covenant Eyes, 1525 West King Street, Owosso, MI 48867, 2010.
5. Bryant, Timothy, "Living Out of Christ," Cornerstone Family Health, Williamsport, PA, 2002.

6. Lutzer, Erwin W., *After You've Blown It*, Multnomah Publishers, Sisters, Oregon. 2004.
7. Ibid p. 25
8. Sherwood, Cyndy, *The Healing Journey*, His Healing Light Ministries, Colorado Springs, CO, 2007.
9. Sherwood, Cyndy, *Roadmap to Healing,* Promised Land Publishing, Colorado Springs, CO. 2009.
10. Sherwood, Cyndy, *The Healing Journey*, His Healing Light Ministries, Colorado Springs, CO, 2007
11. Ibid.

Breinigsville, PA USA
17 February 2011
255781BV00001B/3/P